Beyond Lincoln

A History of Nebraska Hauntings

Beyond Lincoln

A History of Nebraska Hauntings

Tayden Bundy

Beyond Lincoln: A History of Nebraska Hauntings

Copyright © 2018 by Tayden Bundy

Printed in the United States of America

First Edition

Cover design by C Balta
Edited by Karmen Browitt
Printed by University of Nebraska Printing

ISBN 978-1-60962-132-2

Dedicated to
My brother Scotty

Contents

Introduction

Ghost stories have a way of shifting, expanding, and changing over time. With each recounting of a tale the details become less important and the effect the story has on the listener hails over the truth. Discovering the origins of ghost stories is, in many cases, impossible, but occasionally the past creeps into those lost details and finds a way back into the lingering words of the storyteller. I have been listening to these stories all of my life, wondering where they came from and how they manage to live on long past the people who originally created them. Ghosts are the remnants of people who once breathed life into this world and the retelling of the stories connected to them provide a means to keep the history of a community alive.

In Lincoln, driving around town with friends after dark is a tradition amongst teenagers. I remember countless nights filled with ghost stories as we would pass by the houses attached to them or wander through the parks after the sun had set where ghostly figures were known to haunt. The tales included in this book are ones that I have heard hundreds of times from a number of different people, young and old. Ghost stories don't have a shelf life; they become more intriguing the longer they manage to exist. Some of the stories included in this book have been passed down for generations and others are from a time period much closer to the present. Lincoln, like most cities in the United States, has a rich and intriguing history, from the stories of the past, ghosts have emerged in the place of unsolved murders, desperado-type escapes, vigilante justice, catastrophic accidents, and legends generated through false ideas. I chose the stories that I love and continue to share over and over again.

The stories presented here have a history attached to them that, I believe, created tales that have managed to shift over time to be more than what they were originally. All of these places existed once. Although some have changed, they all still hold a presence that continues to ignite the imagination. Wilderness Park was once a bustling attraction for boating and camping enthusiasts, but after the 1930s, the area transformed into a beautiful hiking spot on the outskirts of town. Bloody Mary's house has been gone for decades, burned down by an arsonist who was never caught, but her legend still lingers near the tree line where the house once stood. Seven Sisters Road still remains, isolated in the country, but many of the hills that once lined the road are now leveled farmland. These places along with the others presented here have a history worth sharing. They have a legacy worth passing on.

Keep in mind that the research conducted for this book was done with the ghost stories in mind. I attempted to uncover the details lost through the act of retelling. Of course, this book is a work of fiction on multiple levels, mainly because the information is subjective. The research presented here is the most definitive that I could uncover in relation to the ghost stories that I have heard over and over again throughout my life living in Lincoln, Nebraska. Although I was helped immensely on my journey of discovering the influence of these stories, the true starting point is nearly impossible to find. Stories have a way of creating a life of their own. Ghost stories are wondrous, captivating, and most of all are worth passing on. The history of a place can create a richer experience by providing the opportunity to learn more about the world that surrounds us. I love ghost stories and the history attached to their origins. I hope, in some way, this book allows for a much more thrilling engagement in the tales we have passed down for generations.

20th and Washington

In a quiet Lincoln neighborhood around the southeast corner of 20th and Washington Street, people say you can experience a mysterious cold spot, even on the warmest summer evening. This is the setting for two closely-related ghost stories retold in Lincoln for nearly one hundred years. The streets are lined with enormous trees, most likely the same ones that stood when the tales first originated. Some of the original houses built over a hundred years ago still remain today, exposing a more detailed and unique architecture that has been morphed into a more sleek and boxed design. Both stories include a murder committed by unknown assailants who drove up to an unsuspecting victim innocently passing the day on a stroll or playing with toys as the sun crawled across the sky. Both victims were oblivious to the fact that the last seconds of their lives were coming to an end.

The first tale involves a wealthy young man walking through the neighborhood on a winter night in the early part of the twentieth century. The moon looms high overhead, peeking through the cottonwoods shedding their leaves, as the air grows colder with each passing day. From the north, a roadster speeds down the street, approaching from behind the man as he makes his way toward the southeast corner of the 20th and Washington intersection. As the car approaches, the tires squeal to a stop right next to him. In some versions of the tale, the man speaks to the occupants of the vehicle and then attempts to turn and run; in others, he doesn't have a chance to utter a word. In both versions, however, he is shot twice by one of the people in the car. After the shots are fired, the car speeds away, leaving the man to die on the corner. The noise rings through the neighborhood, causing residents to cautiously exit their homes. When the curious finally approach the man they find him struggling to breathe, clutching his chest. When they ask him what happened, unable to speak, the man attempts to write on the sidewalk in his own blood, most likely to reveal the name of the person who committed the crime. When witnesses are later questioned, no one can provide an accurate description of the car, and the number of people occupying the car changed with each account. The man perished on the corner before he could expose the murderer, leaving behind nothing more than horror stricken bystanders and bloodstained concrete.

In the second tale, a young boy is playing in the neighborhood in the middle of the day. As he approaches the southeast corner of 20th and Washington, a car drives by and someone from inside shoots the boy. In some versions of the story, the car stops just long enough to fire two shots and in others the car simply drives past, firing shots through an open window. After the gunshots, people come out of their homes to see what is going on to find the boy lying on the sidewalk in a pool of his own blood. As they help him and ask him who shot him, the boy tries to write something in his own blood on the concrete, possibly attempting to reveal the person who committed the crime. Like the young man, the boy perishes on the street corner before ever exposing a description of the people in the car.

Today, most people claim to feel a cold spot on the southeast corner of 20th and Washington Street. Even when the person doesn't know which corner to choose, most, if not all, claim that the southeast corner is significantly colder. Others have reported the sounds of disembodied voices and screams in this particular area.

• • •

The truth of this story, however, remains in the details. A documented drive-by shooting did not occur on the southeast corner of 20th and Washington, and another, unsolved murder did occur across the street. On the night of Saturday January 22, 1921, Adrian F. Barstow, the son of a wealthy grain company owner, arrived home after a night out drinking with friends at the University Club in downtown Lincoln. Upon leaving around 11:15 p.m., Barstow offered his friend a ride home because he had been drinking quite heavily. When his friend declined, deciding to walk instead, Barstow drove away. There is a forty-five-minute gap between the time he left the bar and when he finally arrived home around midnight. The whereabouts of Barstow during this time period are unknown. Whether Barstow stopped somewhere along the way or decided to take a detour, the information has never been uncovered. After parking his car in the driveway, Barstow made his way up to the front porch of his house where he lived with his parents and siblings. According to his family, Adrian was heard calling out; "Come out of there!" followed by a gunshot. Adrian was then heard yelling, "Help! Help!" before a second shot was fired, followed by silence. Evidently the first shot hit him in the abdomen and the second shot pierced his left eye. Marjorie Barstow, Adrian's sister, rushed to the front door after hearing the shots and found her brother in the driveway only a few feet from the porch. From her upstairs bedroom window, Adrian's mother, Frances, saw a man ride away on a bicycle. The man was last seen riding across the Barstow front lawn and down Washington Street. Frances described the assailant as a white man of medium build who was wearing a dark overcoat and stocking cap that hid the features of his face. Adrian was still alive in the driveway, but unable to speak and died only a few minutes later as he was being placed in an ambulance.

According to police reports, the assailant lost control and crashed his bike on 19th and "A" Street where he hit a patch of ice. Left behind at the site of the accident was a trail of blood and a flashlight that later was determined to have been stolen from the Barstow home. The police believe he injured his hand or face as a result of the fall. Following the trail of blood led police to 14th and "M" street where they found a large amount of blood, most likely from the shooter stopping to rest, and then the blood trail continued on north of "O" street where all traces disappeared.

After interviews with witnesses, a neighbor returning home in his car noticed a man facing the Barstow home near the entrance of the driveway leaning against a bicycle. The neighbor described the man as tall and slightly built wearing dark clothes and a stocking cap, but not an overcoat. A neighbor in her home across the street claimed to have seen a man wearing an overcoat running away after the shooting. This account, however, omits the use of a bicycle. The police also uncovered testimony in relation to a second assailant seen directly across the street who walked away from the scene of the crime after the shooting took place. After conducting interviews, the police constructed the following three possible occurrences: the murder was premeditated, the murder was a result of a robbery gone wrong or the murderer was on drugs. The key piece of evidence in the case was the flashlight stolen from the Barstow home. The flashlight was found two and half blocks away from the home.

After accessing the scene, police settled on two final theories. The first was the murderer was inside the home attempting to rob the residence when Adrian stepped onto the front porch. Surprised by his presence, the murderer shot Adrian in the stomach, which caused him to fall backward into the driveway and then shot him at close range while on the ground with a .38-caliber pistol, before escaping on a bicycle toward downtown Lincoln. The second theory involved the suspect waiting in the bushes that lined the north side of the driveway for Adrian to arrive home.

Rumors spread after the murder. At the time of the murder, the population of Lincoln was around 55,000, and the publicity involved in the attempt to capture the assailant was widespread. Several newspaper articles over the course of several weeks recounted the event and a high reward, which also drew public attention and hope for a swift capture. One of the rumors was that Adrian was having an affair with one of the neighbor's wives and the murderer was the husband, but this hypothesis was never proven. Another possibility was that Barstow had pulled into the driveway in the midst of a burglary, surprising the burglar who then shot him because Barstow recognized the assailant. Everyone seemed to have a theory about what "really" happened to Adrian Barstow.

Even today, murders, especially unsolved murders, are uncommon in Lincoln, Nebraska. The prominence of the family along with the inability to arrest the shooter allowed for stories to run rampant. Adrian's father, William Townsend Barstow, was President of the Lincoln Grain Exchange. Adrian, a former University of Nebraska student and Lieutenant in the 37th Field Artillery, worked for his father at the time of the murder. The Barstow family name was known throughout Lincoln and the repetitious recounting of the night that took Adrian from the world has continued to baffle and intrigue anyone who has attempted to unravel the mystery.

Narrowing Down the Origins

Several common themes can be connected within the two ghost stories and the unsolved murder of Adrian F. Barstow. The close proximity of the murder in relation to the southeast corner of 20th and Washington Street is, in my opinion, the most important element. The house was directly across the street. Another fact to consider is the crime, itself. The act of murder was almost unheard of in 1921 Nebraska, and the fact that the shooter was never caught only added to the magnitude of the event. Other themes include the fact that a gun was used to shoot Barstow, much like a gun was used to shoot the young man and the young boy.

In both ghost stories the gun is shot twice and the murderer gets away, in the ghost stories this occurs in a car, but the fact that Barstow arrived home in a car could have, over time, changed the use of a bike into another form of transportation.

The combination of an unsolved murder and the prominence of the family most likely created the ghost stories that have been told for generations about the cold spot still felt on the southeast corner of 20th and Washington. Whether that cold spot is the spirit of Adrian F. Barstow will most likely remain unknown. Regardless, a horrible crime was committed within close proximity of where some say you still can feel a chill even on the warmest summer evening.

Wilderness Park

Near the southern edge of town amongst an abundance of trees, running streams, and a creek, several ghost stories weave through miles of trails and make their way into the city of Lincoln. Large groupings of trees tend to provide a sense of disorientation, which can lead to anxiety and fear, posing as a starting point for sinister legends to build momentum. Forests, especially after dark, are full of odd noises seeming to echo from several directions. These areas can also be difficult to maneuver through without a trail to guide the way. The woods can give off an eerie ambience that can be attributed to the possibility of getting lost or discovering a person or place secluded within its depths. All of these elements, along with the creepy nature of the woods have created ghost stories linked to Wilderness Park.

Wilderness Park is an area full of wonder, natural and man-made. Like most places in the United States, the dark forest just outside of town has the ability to create a lingering fog of ghost stories hovering just above the surface of the ground. Wilderness Park is no exception and if any one place could be considered the haunted woods in Lincoln, this area would top the list.

People have experienced multiple levels of paranormal activity in Wilderness Park. Several stories involve seeing ghostly figures ranging from adults to children roaming around the woods. In one prominent story, the apparition of a little girl dressed in white can be seen running until she disappears. Other ghosts are seen passing behind trees to never emerge on the other side or they are noticed standing in the distance only to vanish into thin air. The laughter of children and whispered words indecipherable to the human ear are also heard. Noises associated with a train wreck, such as screeching and clanging metal also can be heard. Most frequently, however, the voices of terror-stricken people echo through the trees. Screams seem to reverberate from all directions. In addition to the abundance of disembodied voices and various sounds, people regularly recount hearing footsteps approaching from behind them near the rail bridge, but when they turn around no one is there.

Another story involves a "witch", living a solitary life in a small cabin in the woods during the early years of the twentieth century. According to legend, several children went missing around 1900, and when the sister of a young boy claimed to have seen her brother being coaxed away by a woman in the area known today as Wilderness Park, the authorities sought her out to question her. After speaking with the woman and searching the area, they uncovered the bodies of several of the children who had recently gone missing. When the woman was questioned, she complained about the children trespassing onto her property and causing disruption. Without substantial evidence to link the old woman to the murders, no arrest or trial ever took place. On account of widespread opinion in relation to a lack of justice, rumors spread throughout town and the locals decided to exact vigilante justice by tracking down the woman, wrapping a chain around her neck, and hanging her from a tree. After her death, her body wasn't found for several weeks.

According to legend, the chain can still be found in the middle of the woods because she is attached to the end, buried beneath the ground. Many say that the sounds of the "Witch of Wilderness Park" can be heard as she struggles to take her last breath over and over again in a residual haunting and the rattling of chains clanking and chiming through the trees. Others swear to hear children, some giggling, others screaming for help as if the witch is still dragging them deeper into the darkness.

• • •

Two distinct historical events took place in Wilderness Park. The first was the Rock Island train wreck in 1894, and the second was the rise and fall of Epworth Park. Both include important moments in the history of Lincoln and provide a backdrop to the origins of the legends and ghost stories of Wilderness Park.

On April 9, 1894, Train No. 8 drawn by Locomotive 213 left Fairbury, Nebraska at 7:30 p.m. on its way to Lincoln. The train consisted of two cars: a combination car for mail, baggage, and passengers, and a single passenger coach. Altogether, the train carried thirty-three passengers and crew. At approximately 9:40 p.m., the train traveling at a high rate of speed reached the trestle bridge on the Rock Island track crossing over the Union Pacific and Burlington tracks forty feet above. Suddenly the train jumped the track, traveled across the ties for about 200 feet, and hurtled over the side of the bridge to the Union Pacific tracks below. The impact instantly killed the engineer and fireman. Moments later the engine caught fire consuming the cars and the wooden bridge.

The sound of the wreck echoed for miles, drawing rescuers from all directions. Authorities, train crew, passengers, and local farmers arrived to pull passengers from the train and douse the flames with fire extinguishers and pails of water from the pond nearby. It was not enough, unfortunately; they were never able to get a steamer over the rough terrain and were left to simply watch the fire burn out on its own. Terror stricken screams emerged from the wreckage as people pinned inside were burned alive. Many people were rescued, but others were consumed in the flames and killed. Once the fire had subsided, an investigation of the area revealed that the fishplates, a piece of metal bolted between two pieces of track to keep them together, were removed to allow the rails to spread under the weight of the locomotive. Pieces of the fishplate, bolts, burrs, and a crowbar were found near the wreckage site and the rails were found dented and gouged where the plates were missing. This evidence indicated the train wreck was not an accident, but an act committed by the hands of an unknown assailant. The wreckage claimed the lives of eleven people and caused injuries to fifteen others.

The condition of the tracks caused immediate suspicion and the motive of the derailment was considered to be a botched robbery attempt. The only suspect for the crime was George Washington Davis. Davis, described as a large African American man, was reportedly seen on the night of the incident running with a lantern along Salt Creek from the wreckage site. Thinking that he was one of the helpers, Davis was called back by a rescuer to assist with pulling people from the train. Once the rails were found altered, suspicions arose as to the whereabouts of Davis who originally had been observed running from the scene. After searching the crowd, Davis was found to have disappeared.

Davis was arrested two days later on a farm about six miles from the city of Lincoln. When detectives asked him why he was at the site of the train wreck, he claimed to have run to the wreckage to help out, after hearing about it while he was at the "colored club" between 8th and 9th and "P" Street in Lincoln. When he was questioned further, however, Davis claimed to have heard the sound of the engine blowing up, which would have occurred long before he managed to run the four miles it took to get there. Although this piece of testimony seemed to imply that Davis was actually at the site of the crash when it occurred, prosecutors found no motive and little evidence to suggest that he actually committed the crime.

Davis never admitted to the crime and remained silent during his trials. During his first trial in March 1895, the jury could not unanimously come to a verdict based on the evidence presented. Davis was taken to trial again in November 1895 and was convicted of second-degree murder and sentenced to twenty years to life in prison. The fact that the verdict was not first-degree would imply that the jury was still uncertain about whether or not he actually was involved in the train wreck. In 1905, Governor John Mickey paroled Davis based on lack of evidence in regard to his conviction and guilt in relation to the crime. Mickey believed that Davis had done his time during his ten years behind bars and deserved freedom based on the outcome of the trial with no true evidence to link him to the train wreck. Upon release, the whereabouts or events in his life thereafter remain unknown. With the exception of the Charles Starkweather murder spree of 1958, the Rock Island train wreck is still one of the largest instances of mass murder in the state of Nebraska, making the crime the largest unsolved murder in the city's history.

Within a decade, the site of the Rock Island train wreck would become an area filled with laughter and enjoyment. Epworth Park located near the south side of 1st and Calvert Streets in Lincoln, Nebraska officially opened in August of 1903. L.O. "Orville" Jones, a delegate to the state Epworth League convention at Nebraska City, proposed construction of the park in 1892. The Methodist Church formed the Epworth Association, a religious organization for youth, in Cleveland in 1889. The group was known for their large camp meetings at Lake Chautauqua, New York and Jones envisioned similar gatherings for the state of Nebraska. Jones was elected president of the conference and was appointed director of Epworth Park.

Upon completion, the park included a dormitory, hotel, four restaurants, an arena with seating for 500 people, and an additional open-air amphitheater, which seated between 2,500 and 3,000 people. The area was fed by the Salt Creek and included a donut-shaped lake for canoe rides and boating. The park also included several small cabins and over 850 tent bases for walk-in tenting that could accommodate 2,500 people. The Burlington Railroad built a spur line that made frequent trips throughout the day to provide transportation to and from Lincoln. The park, resembling a small town in many ways, included several year-round residents who lived in close proximity to a grocery store, bookstore, a bakery, and a post office. Along with programs, theatrical shows, and an adult education movement called Chautauqua, numerous speakers and entertainers visited the park including Billy Sunday, Booker T. Washington, Theodore Roosevelt, Howard Taft, and William Jennings Bryan. Other entertainment included animal acts, magicians, storytellers, singing, dancing, games, and fireworks.

Floods caused by torrential rains in 1935 destroyed the campgrounds, washed away tent sites and ruined buildings, ending the era of gatherings that took place there. After unsuccessful attempts at reviving the park and more floods in the 1940s that destroyed 90 more cabins, covered the ground with silt, and caused damage to the remaining structures, Lancaster County bought the land in 1972 and later named the area Wilderness Park.

Narrowing Down the Origins

Of the types of ghost stories associated with Wilderness Park, the presence of apparitions and the sounds frequently heard seem to relate to the park's history. The noises usually heard involve screaming, crashing metals, and children's laughter. The horrific sounds heard can most likely be attributed to the Rock Island train wreck and the laughter can most likely be linked to the atmosphere created at Epworth Park.

The significance of the train wreck would provide substantial groundwork for the idea that ghosts from the incident haunt the grounds in close proximity of the murders committed at the hands of an individual who was never actually convicted of the crime. Eleven people died in horrific fashion, causing an immediate response from the individuals who lived in and around Lincoln. The fact that the train wreck was in the local paper and a manhunt ensued in an attempt to find the culprit involved in altering the tracks created an atmosphere of anxiety and fear on top of the result of a somber mood on account of the sudden deaths of so many innocent people. The capacity of the event made the incident widespread throughout the state and the fact that the number of people killed is still equal to the largest number of people mass murdered at a single time in Nebraska history can contribute to the overall effect the history has had on the city.

Epworth Park was visited by thousands of people on a daily basis. Laughter filled the air. Such an abundance of people gathered together generates copious amounts of energy. In this case, the energy was positive and could in many ways be linked to the laughter heard amongst the trees today.

The ghost stories involving the witch, however, present multiple issues. First of all, no evidence exists in relation to the disappearances or deaths of several children around the first few decades of the twentieth century at the hands of an old woman who lived in the woods that would eventually become Wilderness Park. In fact, no evidence exists linking to anyone kidnapping or killing multiple children during that time period in or around Lincoln. If children were disappearing at an accelerated rate, especially ones resulting in multiple murders, the incidents would have been known throughout the state. Secondly, the area where the woman was supposed to have lived at that time was a portion of Epworth Park. Although the wooded area is quite large—nearly 1,400 acres—a woman living alone in a shack on the outskirts of town would have been in close proximity to thousands of people on a regular basis. Epworth Park was also equipped with electricity that illuminated that entire area leaving the ability for someone to snatch a child and get away with it much more unlikely, especially if she was burying the children on her land. Trains were running through the area multiple times a day, transporting people to and from Epworth Park. Although the possibility of kidnapping children would have been possible, especially since children were within close proximity to where the witch was supposed to have lived, keeping their disappearances a secret would have been next to impossible.

Most likely the stories in relation to a murderous witch in the woods was derived from tales told around fires late into the night. The children who camped in Epworth Park along with boy scouts and other youth groups could have been warned about the old woman who lived in the woods and would kidnap them if they wandered off too far. These stories, like many others that are told to children to keep them out of danger, could have been produced out of innocent parental involvement and were later formed with the imagination of storytelling children into the dangerous witch who lived in the woods.

Although there is no direct evidence linking a witch to the woods, the truth remains that people hear footsteps coming up behind them when they get close to the bridge where eleven people perished over a hundred years ago. The area that was once the entrance to Epworth Park still holds a daunting atmosphere. The entryway was rebuilt in the 1980s and provides a sense of what it felt like to walk through the large archway into the park. Wilderness Park is open to the public year-round, but don't stay after dark. Not only is doing so restricted by the city, but according to multiple reports, is also forbidden by the spirits that still inhabit the large stretch of wilderness that lines the outer edge of the southwest corner of Lincoln.

Seven Sisters Road

Near the Nebraska and Iowa border, a stretch of road harbors a twisted tale that rambles along the outer edge of a small town. The wide-open space, distance between homes, and darkness surrounding the isolated country roads sets up the perfect place for a ghost story. With moonlight as the only source to light the way, forms can shape in the farmland or dart out from wooded areas before casting shadows in front of car beams and then disappearing into the night. Red eyes appear, glowing as a car passes by. The sounds that echo from wildlife and trees cracking as they twist in the wind can produce a sense of confusion and terror. The story connected to Seven Sisters Road is horrific in nature. The tale has several different versions, but all of them contain the death of seven young women at the hands of one man.

The first iteration of the tale involves a farmer who lived along Seven Sisters Road at the turn of the twentieth century. Along with his wife and seven daughters, the man lived a few miles south of town in a farmhouse. One night the farmer snaps. Several reasons are provided for his sudden burst of anger: one version suggests that the man suspected his wife of cheating on him with a man from town; another claims that the father was drunk and deranged. In either case, one night the farmer drags each of his seven daughters out of the farmhouse one at a time into the dark desolate country. At a distance far enough for screams to be muffled before reaching anyone who could help, the father takes his daughters to seven different trees, atop seven different hills, strings them up by their necks and hangs them.

Another version simply changes the father to the brother committing the heinous acts to his seven sisters. Some versions of the tale have the father or brother hanging the seven young women on seven different trees, atop seven different hills where the road was later constructed. Years after the murder occurred, the county purchased the land. When the country road was built, the seven trees were cut down and some of the hills were leveled out. Now as cars pass over the road, the wheels are driving over the area where the seven sisters were actually hanged. Today, only four hills remain.

According to legend, screams and whispers can be heard near the remaining four hills. The road is known to cause car malfunctions including dimming headlights, freezing speedometers, and windows rolling up and down on their own. The area is also known today as a dead zone for cell service, leaving individuals driving along that stretch of road without connection to the outside world. The most frightening occurrences involve shadowy figures darting out of the darkness, some crossing the road as cars approach, or emerging from the trees. The sound of tinkling bells also can be heard from the abandoned cemetery tucked away in the wooded area near the road. Occasionally, when the moon shines just right, a figure can be seen hanging from a tree atop a hill.

· · ·

Attempting to uncover the origins of this story is rather difficult because no documented evidence exists in relation to a murder of seven young women around the turn of the twentieth century in or around Nebraska City. In fact, no evidence exists of the murder of seven daughters or sisters having occurred on the same night by hanging in all of Nebraska's documented history. Of course, someone potentially could have committed the crimes without being caught, but even during this time period, getting away with such a horrific act would have been next to impossible. First of all, the community was small and census records and land ownership documents kept track of the number of people living in certain areas. Newspapers existed at the time and include reports of much less extreme crimes, which suggests that such a brutal act would not have been easily missed, even in rural Nebraska. With this in mind, uncovering the possibilities of how this story began may be found in the details—in particular, two elements of the story are relevant to discovering how such a story may have begun as something else and later transformed into the ghost story told today.

First of all, the story always contains the deaths of seven women who were either daughters or sisters of the murderer. According to Otoe county census records from the mid-to-late 1800s, a family lived on the stretch of Seven Sisters Road associated with the area that is now known to be haunted about five miles south of Nebraska City. John Warden and his wife Julia purchased land in the Four Mile precinct in 1856. Both were born in Virginia and most likely moved to Nebraska to purchase a large piece of land to build a homestead. John, who recorded his occupation as a farmer, originally owned 160 acres of land and later purchased another 33 acres in 1870. The Wardens grew corn, wheat, potatoes, hay, and orchard products. They also owned livestock including cows, from which they produced butter, and bees, from which they produced honey. John Warden could have been an alcoholic, judging by the numerous recorded arrests for disturbing the peace and public displays of drunkenness, which were reported frequently in the local paper. At the time, drunkenness was not usually recorded in the newspaper, which would imply that his drinking was quite excessive and known by the locals. The most important element related to the Warden family, however, is the number of children they had. John and Julia Warden had seven daughters and one son.

John Warden was likely a drunkard and he did have seven girls, but he definitely did not kill them in a drunken rage because records indicate that all seven daughters have a different date of death and one actually lived until the age of 90. This information also proves that the Warden's only son likewise could not have committed the gruesome murders that became the ghostly tales surrounding Seven Sisters Road. Perhaps the combination of seven daughters and their father's known drunkenness and seemingly violent tendencies created rumors that eventually turned into folklore. Or perhaps a combination of events can be attributed to the overall story.

Vigilante justice made a permanent mark in Nebraska history around the time that the murders in the ghost story are said to have occurred. Between the years 1866 and 1887, five men were hanged at the hands of angry, masked mobs in Nebraska City, making it the town with the most lynching's in the entire state during that time period. One of those five men, Leander "Lee" Shellenberger, lived near Seven Sisters Road.

Lee Shellenberger and his wife, Miranda were arrested for the death of their 11-year-old daughter, Margaret "Maggie" Catherine Shellenberger, on April 29, 1886. Through court records, witness testimony, and evidence collected from the scene of the crime, information in relation to the murder spread across the state of Nebraska. The Shellenbergers, like the Wardens, lived approximately five miles south of Nebraska City on a farm. Lee was well-known in Nebraska City as a saloon operator.

Evidence suggests that Maggie Shellenberger's father and stepmother abused her. Maggie had run away from home several times and two days before the murder took place Maggie, along with her older brother Joseph, had escaped again. After searching for them on horseback, their father found them nine miles from home. Once he located his children, he forced them to walk all the way back while he rode behind them. Upon arriving home, Lee supposedly threatened to cut his daughter's throat if she ran away again, whipping and kicking her as punishment.

Little record exists in relation to Lee Shellenberger's trial, most likely because he was swiftly convicted, but Miranda went to trial six months after Lee was sentenced to be hanged on December 9, 1886, finally exposing elements relating to the crime in greater detail. Several people testified during the trial including her stepson Joseph. According to Joe, on April 29, 1886, his father went down the road to a neighbors' house to get potatoes. While his father was away, his stepmother directed Maggie to clean the cellar stairs with a knife to remove the mud caked on them. Leaving Maggie in the house, Miranda went out to the barn to retrieve eggs. At this time, Joe was in the barn with his stepmother cleaning the stables. While they were still in the barn, Lee returned and a verbal dispute occurred about Lee being gone too long. Lee instructed Joe to retrieve the pony that was grazing near the barn and then began walking back toward the house with Miranda. A few moments later, Miranda called out to Joe to go to the neighbor's house for help because Maggie had cut her throat. Joe left without ever entering the house.

According to the neighbor who was summoned by Joe, he found Miranda on the porch upon arrival. After asking where Maggie was, she told him that Maggie was in the cellar. The neighbor then went inside the Shellenberger home where he found Lee at the cellar door with a lamp and they descended the stairs together. The neighbor found Maggie's body lying halfway in a wooden box. He described Maggie's throat as being cut in four different places and the floor and walls were covered in blood. The neighbor then helped Lee carry the body up to a second-story bedroom where they placed her on a bed. Upon further investigation of the cellar, a butcher's knife was found, which had been lying on the floor near Maggie as she lay in the box.

After a physician examined the body, he recorded four distinct cuts that had severed the windpipe and carotid arteries. Maggie was buried on May 1, 1886, but was later exhumed on June 9 for further medical examination. The second physician recorded three distinct incisions, one near the chin, which severed the windpipe and all blood vessels, and another set that went all the way to the back of the neck severing the carotid artery twice.

According to the second physician, either cut would likely have caused instant death, which would make self-inflicting the second cut impossible. The cuts also indicated the strength of the person inflicting them was much greater than Maggie.

When Miranda took the stand to testify, she recounted a similar story told by her stepson Joe, and then exclaimed that her husband was to blame for the murder. Miranda claimed that she stopped to clean off her shoes while Lee went inside the house. After hearing a scream, Miranda entered the house to find Lee coming up from the cellar covered in blood. Lee told her that he had cut Maggie's throat after she called him names. When Miranda tried to go to help Maggie, she was stopped and Lee told her that if she said a word, he would kill her too. Lee then forced her to swear that she would tell anyone who asked that Maggie had committed suicide and to have Joe get the neighbor. Miranda was acquitted on all counts and faded into obscurity.

Lee's execution was scheduled for March 25, 1887, but it was postponed after his lawyer was able to get the case to the Supreme Court. The delay and possible overturning of Lee's conviction sent a shock through the community and they decided to take justice into their own hands. On the morning of July 25, 1887, a mob of angry locals armed with guns and clubs arrived at the Nebraska City jail and demanded to be allowed to enter. Once they were refused, they broke through the door and iron cage.

While inside, a few men entered the sheriff's office, which was directly above Shellenberger's cell. After cutting a hole through the floor, they dropped a ladder down and hauled him up through the opening. After dragging him out to the courthouse yard, they threw a rope up into the nearest tree, looped the other end around Shellenberger's neck, and asked him if he had anything to say. Shellenberger declared his innocence and simply asked that his body be returned to his birthplace in Virginia where he wanted to be buried on his father's farm. The mob then strung him up and dropped him down several times. Each time he was asked if he was guilty and upon continuing to claim innocence they pulled him up again. After the sixth time, he was hauled up one final time and choked to death. According to witnesses, Shellenberger's last words were, "I'll haunt you for this!"

Narrowing Down the Origins

Finding common links between the ghost story and the history of Otoe County seems to provide the clearest answers as to how this particular story was created. The most important element to consider is that no documented evidence exists in relation to the murders or deaths of seven young women who were all related around the mid-to-late 1800s and who all died at the same time under unorthodox circumstances. The location of the Warden farmstead and the fact that the family had seven daughters and one son is an obvious connection to the ghost story, but the most closely related crime—a father killing his own daughter—connects it even more readily with the Shellenberger murder.

The close proximity of the road in relation to the Shellenberger family is also important to consider because of two elements: murder of a daughter and lynching. Although major discrepancies exist in relation to the ghost story, such as the fact that only Maggie Shellenberger was murdered and Lee Shellenberger was lynched, not on his own land, but in the courthouse yard, the details suggest a connection when considering the time period and place of the murder. There is no evidence to show whether or not the Wardens and the Shellenbergers lived in the same area at the same time, but their timelines do come relatively close when looking at the last known documentation of their residence in Otoe County. John Warden was reported to have left Nebraska after the death of his wife in 1880 and returned to his home in Virginia, but he was actually buried in the cemetery on the land once owned by the Wardens in 1901. Since the murder of Maggie occurred in 1886, only a six-year gap separates the two families and could mean that both did, in fact, live in the same area at the same time. Another interesting connection is that both the Wardens and Lee Shellenberger hailed originally from Virginia.

Another link can be made with the frequent arrests and bulletins in the newspaper of John Warden's drunkenness. One version of the ghost story involves the death of seven daughters at the hands of an intoxicated father. The fact that locals presumably knew about John Warden's behavior, the number of daughters he had, and later the murder and lynching of Shellenberger who lived near his land and was a saloon owner could have potentially interconnected such stories. At the simplest level, although not documented, Warden, during one of his drunken tirades, could have commented on committing such an act in public even though he never actually did.

Lee Shellenberger was also a well-known saloon operator in Nebraska City and had on one occasion shot a man in the back of the head. According to a brief newspaper article, the injury inflicted by Shellenberger caused no harm to the man, identified only as Johnson, and Shellenberger claimed that he was drunk at the time. This incident occurred in 1880, the year that Warden left for Virginia, but there is no evidence that shows they both lived in the same area during that time. The fact that Shellenberger shot a man while drunk could also carry some weight when trying to connect the drunkenness in the ghost story to the actual truth about the men who once lived within the area where the story originated.

Although no historical evidence can be found directly linking to the ghost story murders, the coincidence of all of the details related to the residences in close proximity to the road has intriguing similarities. Over time, these details could have gradually shifted into the ghost story known today. In any case, numerous reports of ghost activity along Seven Sisters Road have been recorded and the possibility of a mass murder, although unlikely, could have occurred.

Bloody Mary

Almost every town has a terrifying tale about the old woman who lives alone in the house on the outskirts of town, the exterior walls eroding, chipping paint, and exposing the wooden bone frame beneath. The yard is described invariably as unkempt, overgrown with unruly weeds and uncut grass, which blocks the view of the home from the road. In Lincoln, that woman is Bloody Mary. Some places become a rite of passage for teenagers to trespass upon to leave their mark and to talk about into their old age. The large farmhouse near 44th and Superior was the place to go for youth growing up in Lincoln, Nebraska. The wooded area east of the property became a "lovers' lane," where teenagers would sit with their partners as the moon slipped down below the western skyline and drink alcohol far away from the eyes of local law enforcement. Unfortunately, destruction and theft of the house and harassment of the woman who lived inside only a few hundred yards away became a ritual. Young people from town would drive out in the middle of the night to throw rocks at her windows, break in to steal trophies, and taunt the woman who occupied the residence.

The ghost stories surrounding Bloody Mary involve a distorted history morphed into folklore. Legends begin with a bit of mystery. The tales involve a ghostly figure wandering the land that was once owned by the Partington family. A tall woman, dressed in a white overcoat, lurks amongst the trees and emerges to frighten trespassers. The sounds of gunshots can be heard echoing through the woods, followed by screams. Other stories involve a witch who buried bodies on her land and who now protects her ill deeds. In some versions, the lost souls beneath the soil, roam the surrounding area, trying to find their way home. The enormous old farmhouse that once stood on the property also has a haunting presence. On the night of October 26, the ghostly outline of the house that once stood dominating over the countryside can be seen if the weather is just right. Finally, Bloody Mary can be summoned by chanting her name three times into a mirror in a darkened room. After calling out for her, she appears either in the mirror or in the reflection directly behind the person.

• • •

Historical evidence projects a much different picture. Mary Ann Partington, the woman who would come to be known as Bloody Mary, was born on March 22, 1889 in Lincoln, Nebraska. She was the first child of Ella and Harold James Partington, who had eight more children between 1889 and 1904. Mary was born into the infancy of Lincoln, which had been incorporated for only two years at the time and was still a rural, wide-open space. In 1906, Mary and her family moved into the home where she would live for over seventy years.

The Partingtons built their farmhouse "nine rods" east of Salt Creek. The house was enormous for the time period with six bedrooms, two parlors, a recreation room, and a 3,000 gallon storage tank that was filled with water pumped from a windmill. Underground pipes also supplied the home and barn with cold and hot water. The pond on the property, deemed Partington Lake, attracted neighbors and people from nearby Lincoln who would go fishing in the summer and ice skating in the winter. Visitors were allowed to hunt on the property with expressed permission of the family. The family also entertained friends and family with gatherings and parties where everyone would mingle on the wrap-around porch and watch the construction of the State Capitol Building and the firework shows that took place at Capitol Beach.

By the age of twenty-one, Mary received her teaching certificate and taught in various schools throughout Nebraska, Minnesota, and Wyoming. She later graduated from the University of Nebraska after only three years with a Bachelors of Arts with a major in English. In addition, she also received a Teacher's College Diploma and University Teacher Certificate. She continued to teach in Nebraska for several years until her mother fell ill in 1922.

After the death of Mary Partington's mother Ella in 1923, Mary moved back into her childhood home to help her father. She continued working as a substitute teacher, helped with local events, volunteered, taught for the 4-H club, and held family reunions. She was a social person who helped the community through education, and she entertained others with her engaging personality. Friends and family described her as a headstrong woman who shared her opinions and loved to tell stories.

After her father's health began to fail, he rented out parts of his land. One family rented a section of land covered in trees north of the Partington home. The two brothers used the property for their garbage pickup business. They purchased pigs to eat the garbage and hired a man to tend to the pigs, who would come to be known as "Pigman" by local teenagers who used the area near Salt Creek as a place to congregate after dark. With the onset of this new local legend, hordes of youth began going out into the desolate area shrouded in mystery.

On July 6, 1944, Harold passed away, leaving the house to Mary. For several years she lived without much trouble, but in the 1950s the city began to expand and the area north of the Partington home was sold for development. Neighborhoods and businesses filled the once-empty landscape with people. Along with the expansion of Lincoln, Mary began experiencing varying degrees of harassment by local youth, who from the appearance of the house and the eccentric nature of Mary, may have believed the house was unoccupied. The use of the secluded dead end road that led out to the woods provided the route whereby teenagers drove past the seemingly abandoned home, causing a stir of rumors to spread about who lived inside, which in turn provoked an abundance of dares and initiations. The darkness of the house that was absent of electricity provided a sense of dread and mystery.

Stories spread about the secluded woman who was said to wear a long white housecoat and the ghostly shapes that could be seen in the windows from shadows cast by oil lamps and candles. Once word was spread, fraternity houses from the University of Nebraska began initiating new members with dares of running up to the porch and knocking on the door, throwing rocks at the house, or calling out to get her to come to her bedroom window. Mary remained silent for several years about the harassment she received, but on the night of October 25, 1961, the level of menace reached far beyond simply calling out and throwing rocks.

A call came into to the Lancaster County Sheriff's Office reporting a shooting and a man lying in the yard of the Partington home. Upon investigation, the officers called to the scene found no evidence of a disturbance let alone a shooting after searching the yard and road near the home. The truth is that a man was not shot that night on the Partington farm, but Mary in fact was. A .22-caliber rifle slug had torn through the walls of the house and hit Mary in the stomach. The call to the police did not come from Mary, but she did state that she heard the police car around 10:00 p.m. and watched them simply circle the yard and drive off as she tried to draw their attention by calling out from her bedroom window. The officers never once knocked on the door to ensure that the woman who lived inside was uninjured. Mary stated that she did not know who called in the shooting because at the time she did not own a telephone. The next day a stranger knocked on her door to ask for assistance in recovering her dog that had run away. Upon discovering Mary's injuries, the woman took her to Saint Elizabeth Hospital in Lincoln where she was treated and released. The police later stated that they believed that a trespasser most likely shot at the house believing it to be unoccupied. The person who shot Mary that night was never caught. After being shot, Mary acquired a gun of her own.

After purchasing a telephone, Mary called in numerous accounts of harassment and vandalism over the course of several years to the Lancaster County Sheriff's Office. She called in reports of shots fired at her house, burglary, broken windows, red painted obscenities defacing the outside of her home, fires on her porch, and a tree being cut down in her yard, along with the regular trespassers who called out and lingered on her front yard. Mary even took her mailbox indoors each night to ensure that it would not be stolen or knocked down by morning. At one point Mary was tied up in her home by an intruder who demanded food and money, once he received what he came for he left Mary alone in the house.

Mary eventually used her gun on the frequent trespassers. On September 18, 1964, Mary found several cars parked in her yard after hearing a noise close to midnight. After ordering them to leave, rocks were thrown at her window as they yelled up at her. In an attempt to get them to leave, Mary fired a shot from her second-story bedroom window. The five teenagers in her yard scattered and ran back toward their cars, but not everyone escaped unscathed. The shotgun pellets hit an eighteen-year-old girl sitting in the backseat of one of the cars. The girl suffered wounds to the chest, shoulder, and neck, but survived. Mary was never charged for the shooting because the teenagers were trespassing on her property and vandalizing her home.

The event that most likely contributed to the name Bloody Mary occurred during the early morning hours of October 26, 1966. After being awakened by sounds of a break-in around 3:00 a.m., Mary grabbed her shotgun, proceeded downstairs, and called the police. After hanging up the phone, she heard a window break. Following the sound, she made her way into the kitchen where she found an intruder attempting to enter the home through the broken window. A flash sparked through the darkened house as Mary fired the gun. When police arrived they found Eldon Hill, a former mental patient from Iowa, lying face up beneath the kitchen window with a large hole in his right cheek. No charges were ever filed against Mary for the death of Hill, but the incident provoked the notion that Mary was, in fact, as terrifying as the tales made her out to be.

The dares and initiations continued and seemed to accelerate over time. What started out as running up and knocking on the door eventually progressed into entering and exiting the house before Mary caught the intruder, sometimes stealing something from the home to prove they had actually been inside. Several people boasted about the trophies they had acquired from a successful dare to take one of Mary's possessions.

Around the age of 86, when her health began to fail and she could no longer take care of herself alone, Mary finally moved out of her family home in 1976. Once the house was finally truly abandoned, vandals stripped the home of everything that was left behind, including all of the woodwork. In one last act of terrorizing a woman who had been known by most as a generous and welcoming person, an unknown arsonist burned down the Partington home on June 23, 1977. Not long after the fire, the house was razed. Although the structure disappeared into the land, the legend continued on. Mary Ann Partington died on June 12, 1979 in Lincoln, Nebraska and her legacy as an unconventional and frightening entity has managed to haunt the north side of town ever since.

Narrowing Down the Origins

Bloody Mary was created by active imaginations. Mary Ann Partington was an eccentric woman who lived alone for several years. The fact that Mary never married, openly expressed her opinions, lived without electricity and modern conveniences, and resided in a large home on a dead end road generated the perfect combination of elements to construct a terrorizing legend. And a legend was all it was. Mary was a devoted daughter, sister, and friend. She educated students for decades and was involved in social events and gatherings that attracted people from all over town. The stories of a ghostly figure haunting the grounds where the Partington farmhouse once stood may very well be true, but the sinister characteristics of the woman who lingers on carry little to no merit. The fact that Mary lived alone in a large house with no electricity seems to be the most profound reason as to why these legends began. The mystery surrounding Mary to the teenagers, who harassed her for several years along with the death of Eldon Hill, ignited the folklore.

The origins linked to the use of a mirror to invoke the spirit of Bloody Mary can most likely be attributed to another urban legend associated with Mary Tudor who was Queen of England and Ireland from 1553 to 1558. She obtained the moniker "Bloody Mary" after she executed hundreds of Protestants. The use of a mirror to bring forth the ghost is well-known throughout the United States. Teenagers have been using the ritual to terrify friends at sleepover parties for decades. After Mary Partington was given the same name, the idea of conjuring her spirit was most likely transformed to fulfill the local tale.

At the end of the day, however, Mary should be remembered for her kind and giving nature and not for the horrendous rumors and unruly behavior brought on by teenagers that caused her incredible strife. Bloody Mary can live on in our imaginations as the ghost that haunts the heartland, but never forget the true history behind the legend.

Barnard Park

Nestled in the center of a historic district in Fremont, Nebraska is a park with a long and interesting history. Walking through the black wrought iron archway into the grassy areas of a pristine recreational area, one would never know that members of the Mormon Trail used the site frequently, or that the ground was once the site of a cemetery. Surrounded by some of the first homes built in the town, the park is a focal point with an intriguing past.

A common ghost story associated with Barnard Park involves a grief stricken mother who arrived in the town that would later become Fremont in the 1840s along with other travelers of the Mormon Trail. While staying in a camp, the young daughter of the woman died. Unable to leave her child behind, the woman stayed and according to legend, never left the site of the area that is now the park. During winter months, the woman can be seen late at night, walking around the park crying. She is usually seen as transparent in nature and disappears or fades into the cold night air.

Other ghost stories include the apparition of a man sleeping on a park bench. When someone approaches the man, he disappears. Another report involves a couple of friends who stopped at the park after dark. While sitting under the gazebo they heard footsteps approaching, but when they looked around, they saw nothing. Spooked by the sounds, they decided to leave. As they were walking out of the park, they heard the footsteps again except when they turned around this time, they saw the figure of a man walking toward them, his face absent of any features. Even under the streetlights, the face was indistinguishable. They ran from the park and never turned back to see if the man followed them out.

The sounds of disembodied voices and children screaming can be heard throughout the park. Some visitors have even experienced being pushed or touched by an unseen hand and feel as if they are being watched. Others have witnessed one of the swings in the playground moving on windless nights. Most of the paranormal instances are reported to occur at night, leaving most people to venture out only in the daylight. In addition to the paranormal experiences within the park grounds, many of the historic homes surrounding the park are also said to be haunted. One evening, just before sunset, a small group of women were walking through the park when another woman, who they did not know, approached them. They engaged in conversation for a few moments before the woman crossed the road to a house bordering the park. They watched as she walked up the porch steps and knocked on the door. When no one answered after a few moments, the woman walked through the closed door and disappeared.

. . .

Before Fremont, Nebraska was officially incorporated, large groups of people on the Mormon Trail passed through the area and some set up a temporary camp. The Great Mormon Migration took place between 1846 and 1847 as a means to express religious freedom in another part of the country. Joseph Smith founded the Mormon religion on April 6, 1830 in Fayette, New York and would later be considered a prophet among Mormons. Guided by an angel, Smith claimed to have found buried gold plates, which he translated into the Book of Mormon. The Mormon Migration began as a result of religious persecution. Smith had believed that Nauvoo, Illinois would be a place that the Mormons could settle permanently, but because of polygamy and the sudden growth of the church, locals became agitated, and on June 27, 1844 an angry mob killed both Joseph Smith and his brother Hyrum in Carthage, Illinois. After Smiths' death, a man named Brigham Young became his successor and encouraged the Mormon population to still consider the plans Smith had shared to move west. After continuing to be persecuted in Nauvoo by means of locals burning down homes and farms, the migration finally began. The Mormon population decided to move to the Salt Lake region of Utah and by 1846 the migration was underway. Brigham

Young and other Mormon people arrived in, what would later become, the city of Fremont on April 16, 1847, where they set up Fremont Camp. At the time of their arrival, the company included 143 men, 3 women, 2 children, and 73 wagons. The members of the Mormon Trail Migration would reach the valley of the Great Salt Lake on July 24, 1847. Throughout the course of the migration, 6,000 people died and were buried in various locations along the way.

Fremont, Nebraska was platted in 1856. E. H. Barnard, one of the town founders and surveyor, laid out the area for the site of the town. The first boundaries of the city were from J Street on the west, Union Street on the east, First Street on the south, and Twelfth Street on the north. The town was officially incorporated in 1859. A city park and Green Grove Cemetery were established around 1860. Ridge Cemetery was established in 1878, after Green Grove Cemetery became overcrowded. The bodies from Green Grove Cemetery were transported and reburied in Ridge Cemetery west of the town. According to legend, some of the bodies were never found because many were buried in unmarked graves and were left behind. Some of the bodies were most likely from the Mormon Trail Migration members who had passed through the area and set up a camp near the site of Green Grove Cemetery. Today the park has received the moniker "Dead Man's Park" by the locals because of the probability that some bodies still remain on the site. In the mid-1880s, the area that was once Green Grove Cemetery became Barnard Park.

Barnard Park was named after E. H. Barnard. Barnard came to Nebraska in 1856 with John. A. Koontz and claimed land in what would later become Fremont. Barnard and Koontz built a log cabin, which was the first building ever built in the city of Fremont. At the time there were other buildings, but they were located outside of the cities boundaries. The log cabin was originally built as a residence, but later became a boardinghouse and a hotel. Barnard was responsible for laying out the town, but later focused on farming, held several local offices including President of the City Council, County Treasurer of Dodge County, and served in the State Legislature. Later in life, he was involved in the real estate business, loans, and insurance.

Barnard Park is the central feature to the Barnard Park Historic District. Surrounded by some of the first homes constructed in the city of Fremont by the business and professional community, the park is a landmark and focal point of the city. The park includes a playground, sitting areas, and a beautiful gazebo. The area is open to visitors year-round and offers a peaceful experience for a picnic or spending time with friends and family. After dark, however, the tranquil nature of the park seems to shift and ghostly figures take over the area seemingly appearing out of thin air.

Narrowing Down the Origins

The most notable ghost story involving the woman from the Mormon Trail Migration seems to provide the clearest image to the origins of the legends surrounding Barnard Park. The multitudes of people who made the trek during the mid-1800s experienced difficult travel, which resulted in the deaths of several thousand people. The possibility that some of those travelers were buried in or near Fremont Camp is very likely, and the story of the woman who stayed behind after her daughter died is also plausible. The grief that one would feel during such an incredible and enduring journey after losing a child and leaving behind a loved one would be incredibly difficult. The idea that the woman heard crying today is an individual from the migration makes sense and could very well be from a true story that has been lost amongst the folklore.

The fact that the park was originally a cemetery, seems too provide an important background into the existence of supernatural occurrences. The sounds heard at night in the park could be those left behind when all of the other bodies were removed. Not only were those graves left unmarked, never providing a name to the body once laid to rest there, but also the idea of being abandoned provides a reason for the ghostly sounds. The apparition of the man sleeping on the bench, however, remains a mystery. No records exist involving the death of a man on a park bench, and discovering the origins of this particular apparition are yet to be found. There are, however, reports of people found sleeping in the park that have scared visitors enough to call the local police to have them removed. Such events potentially could have turned into ghost stories to caution people from visiting the park at night. The instances of being physically touched or pushed are also difficult to link to historical evidence. These interactions could be residual instances linking to the Mormon Trail Migration or to an incident yet to be shared linking the park to violence. As far as the history of the park suggests, however, there have been no violent actions recorded to have occurred within the park grounds.

Although the park is open to the public, keep in mind that the historic district surrounding the area has a rich and intriguing history with residence in close proximity to the park. The city of Fremont, like all cities in Nebraska, has a past worth sharing. Be mindful of the local residents and the importance of such an amazing landmark situated in the heart of such a beautiful city. Whether or not the ghosts are from the distant past or from a time much closer to the present, the park is still a place where people gather to share memories, ones that someday might remain as laughter echoing through the black wrought iron archway and out into the city.

Norfolk Regional Center

Asylums are notorious places for hauntings. Over the course of time, the methods used to treat patients has evolved, but many of those approaches created unbelievable outcomes, some altering the person involved permanently. Certain horrors arise from imaging these types of procedures occurring, which can create daunting images of the institutions that implemented them. Many of the patients were considered to be the outcasts of society, set apart from others based on their mental state and some of those people were left behind, never to be released back into society after being placed in an institution. Norfolk Hospital for the Insane would become one of those places, surrounded in mystery and plagued by various newspaper reports involving suicide, unorthodox treatment of patients, abusive staff, fires, and even murder.

Several supernatural encounters have been reported inside the many buildings on the property. One night a registered nurse was conducting a building check when she heard loud moaning in the first floor entrance of the pharmacy and clinic areas. After calling another employee to confirm the noise and to ensure what she heard was real, she searched for the source of the sound. She eventually came upon a patient's room with the door closed. When she opened the door, she found the room empty, but the moaning became louder, causing her to quickly shut the door and leave. Later in the medical clinic, she consulted with day staff about the sound and they confirmed that a patient had recently died in the room where the moaning had originated.

Another Norfolk Regional Center worker used the underground tunnels that connected the buildings to transport supplies. The tunnels were used for numerous reasons including transporting patients, food, and other materials used within the various buildings. While making her way through one of the tunnels, all of the lights suddenly turned off, leaving her in complete darkness, unable to even see her hand in front of her face. After deciding which direction to go, she continued on toward the building that needed the supplies, using the wall to guide her along the way. The woman felt disoriented, and noises began echoing from the direction she had come. When she called out to see if another worker had come to help, she received no reply. Frightened by the sounds, she quickly made her way to the other end of the tunnel. Bursting through the door, she found that the only area in darkness was the tunnel that seemed to continue on without end.

After Norfolk Regional Center was closed, some of the buildings were used as public housing. A woman had numerous supernatural experiences while living in the building that previously housed doctors who worked at the facility. The first apparition she saw was in the basement. While the resident was doing laundry, a transparent woman, wearing a long dress, walked passed the doorway to the laundry room. After the first appearance, the apartment tenant saw the apparition multiple times near the same area until she moved out several years later. Another evening, the same tenant was in the area of the basement where the walls were lined with storage units. As she was locking up her belongings, a feeling of dread fell over her. She quickly finished what she was doing and headed toward the stairs where she was hit with a gust of wind. After her experience near the stairs, she began seeing a tall thin man in a black suit in her apartment and odd noises started occurring each night. The apparition of the man would open the living room closet door. When she later described the male apparition to another co-worker, they affirmed that the man she was seeing was a doctor who used to live in the building. At night, she felt as if objects were being thrown on her bed. Another tenant in the apartment building experienced feeling as if someone was breathing on their neck while in their bathroom, and someone saw an apparition who was hanging from a rope in one of the corners of the basement.

Apparitions were reported wandering through the halls of the Norfolk Regional Center only to disappear around a corner and into a dead end. Visitors have reported hearing screams, footsteps, and knocking noises. Doors frequently opened and closed and the lights flickered off and on, especially in the underground tunnel system. Objects were reported flying across the room, and televisions turned off and on. A woman could be heard crying on the third floor of the building that later became an apartment complex after the institution was shutdown. Long after the building was closed and condemned, several people still reported feeling as if they were being watched by someone from the upper windows of the main building. Others simply feel uneasy and sad while on the grounds.

• • •

The history of the Norfolk Regional Center may shed some light on the existence of the ghostly figures that roam the grounds, which were previously inhabited by thousands of patients over nearly a 100 year timespan. The construction of what was originally called the Norfolk State Hospital for the Insane began on March 8, 1885, after a legislative act provided funding for a new hospital that would be located three miles from Norfolk, Nebraska. At the time, two other hospitals were already operating in Hastings and Lincoln, Nebraska. The facility was built on 320 acres of land, and the structures on-site included a large, four-story brick building, which consisted of administrative offices, parlors, and officers' quarters. In addition, 96 rooms for patients, dining rooms, bathrooms, and attendants' rooms were included in the original construction. Two years later, two wings were added to the main building along with a kitchen, bakery, chapel, boilers, engine, pump, and barn. The facility officially opened on February 15, 1888 with 97 patients filling the building to capacity. Another building was added in 1897, allowing for an additional 104 patients and in 1898, more rooms were added allowing for another 300 patients.

Patients were diagnosed with various mental illnesses throughout the facilities long history, but most people were temporarily institutionalized for such diagnoses as emotional instability related to heartbreak, financial difficulties, domestic troubles, overwork, sunstroke, jealousy, and heredity among various other life events and troubles that would be linked to depression today. Patients with drug and alcohol addiction were also admitted. Other patients exhibited signs of dementia and Alzheimer's. Some of the treatments used in the past such as sterilization that occurred after 1918 and electroshock therapy were used alongside more traditional treatments such as recreational and occupational therapy.

Only a few years after opening, a devastating fire consumed all but one building. On September 23, 1901, a fire started in the underground tunnels. At the time of the fire, 300 patients, both male and female lived in the facility, along with 40 attendants and workmen. Around 4:30 a.m. a night watchman discovered flames and smoke coming from the tunnel near Ward E. Unfortunately, the water supply for the facility was insufficient to douse such a large fire and the water store was exhausted within a half-hour. When the volunteer fire department arrived, they found the firefighting apparatus unusable because the hose connection was not a standard size, which prohibited the use of the city water supply. Many of the patients were initially locked in their rooms until order was restored and they were released to the grounds surrounding the facility. Some patients refused to leave their rooms and had to be forced out of the building. Several patients ran away, but were later found. Only a few patients were seriously hurt or burned and two patients died. Victor Kosper of Colfax County, Nebraska was taken to safety, but ran back in twice before being found and taken back out. After running in a third time, Kosper died while in his room. Another patient, W. E. Jasperson was pulled from his window after rescuers broke the grating that was preventing him from escaping the flames. Although he was rescued from the building, Jasperson later died in the hospital as a result of the burns he received. The quick response from attendants and staff and the bravery of those men and women who went back to save patients are the sole reason for the few deaths that occurred that night. Also, the majority of the furniture and bedding was saved from the women's department because that building was the last to burn. Most of the buildings, however, were consumed. By 11 o'clock the next morning, all but one building remained as onlookers watched the fire finally fizzle out on its own. Special trains were sent to Norfolk to transport 200 patients to Lincoln and the rest to Hastings. Two reasons were provided for the origin of the fire, but the true reason remains unknown. The first was that rats had gnawed the insulation of the wires in the tunnel. The second reason was a steam pipe became overheated in the tunnel that contained all of the main lines for steam, water, and electric light wiring. Either way, the Norfolk State Hospital for the Insane lay in ruins and two patients lost their lives.

Throughout the existence of the Norfolk State Hospital for the Insane, multiple deaths occurred on the property ranging from suicide to murder. Other accidental deaths of both patients and staff occurred as well. The history of the hospital also includes a few controversial issues related to the treatment of patients and the conditions in which they lived. On February 13, 1889, a kitchen employee died during an abortion procedure at the facility's hospital. On Christmas Eve in 1906, a man committed suicide by cutting his throat. The patient managed to pick the lock on his room and broke into a closet, where he found a razor blade. By the time the attendant found him five minutes later, the man had died as a result of the cuts inflicted on his throat. On April 24, 1907, a day nurse in the women's infirmary burned to death after a small alcohol lamp exploded, igniting her clothing. Attempts to smother the flames failed and she died six hours later as a result of her extensive burns. On May 4, 1907, a patient was found hanging from the ceiling in the cellar of one of the buildings. On May 27, 1915, a patient died as a result of injuries inflicted during a scuffle with attendants. After refusing to hitch up a team of horses, the patient became aggravated and fell to a cement floor of a horse barn during an altercation with an attendant. As a result of the fall, the patient fractured his skull, causing him to die three days later. On February 24, 1929, a patient took her own life by hanging herself with a stocking in her ward. By the time the nurse discovered the patient, she was already gone. On February 26, 1933, a patient burned to death after a haystack caught fire. The patient was smoking a pipe and fell asleep, causing his clothes to catch fire. The flames ignited the hay he was resting on and spread quickly. On October 25, 1996, a patient shot a doctor in his office and was able to fire at several other people in a hallway before being detained, which resulted in another employee being shot in the leg. The doctor died in the hospital and the other employee was treated and released.

The Norfolk Hospital for the Insane operated for nearly a hundred years. In 1920, the facility's name was changed to the Norfolk State Hospital and was changed again in 1970 to the Norfolk Regional Center. In 1955, at the hospitals peak, the facility housed over 1,300 patients. In addition to various jobs offered to patients within the facility, many holiday celebrations were held throughout the years along with movie showings, plays, and dances. The facility also had a chorus and orchestra. The Norfolk Regional Center officially closed in 1980, but was later used for a sex offender treatment program and was eventually converted into an apartment complex. The remaining building of the Norfolk Regional Center was demolished in the summer of 2016.

Narrowing Down the Origins

Most of the people who worked in the Norfolk Regional Center speak highly of the staff and the treatment of patients. Many mental institutions receive a stigma related to fear and uneasiness. These feelings can be attributed to the fact that science and medical treatments for individuals with mental disabilities have evolved significantly over the last 100 years, and some of the treatments used on patients caused traumatic results. Women were institutionalized under conditions that would be unheard of today, such as hysteria, rebelliousness, and acting beyond their role as women. Experimental treatments like lobotomies have a lasting impact because of the significant damage done to the individuals who received the treatment. Many facilities housed people who were difficult to understand or exhibited behaviors unknown or were misunderstood during certain time periods in history. Many people, especially in the first half of the twentieth century were simply left behind in mental facilities. Some individuals who were abandoned simply lived out the rest of their lives in such institutions. Mental hospitals can be traumatizing to people who never actually live or work in them. Most people have been driven to believe that madness runs rampant in the halls and that violence amongst patients and staff is common. The truth, however, is most patients were not abused, neglected, or murdered. Most were treated and later released to live normal lives, and many of the patients who stayed, came to call the facility home. Although the Norfolk Regional Center has a past occasionally composed of fires, mistreatment of patients, suicide, and murder, these events were few in comparison to the help and security patients received over its long and compelling existence. Another important element to consider is that some of the buildings lay vacant for nearly 40 years. Abandoned buildings are full of mystery and can lead to stories being told, especially by individuals who trespass and find themselves inside a run-down building with echoing hallways and an unsettling atmosphere. The reason behind the lasting legacy of the Norfolk Regional Center remains unknown, but those spirits that remain on the grounds may simply be the ones who never left a place they once called home.

Grasshopper Hill

A tiny cemetery dotted with faded white crosses and worn markers sit upon a hill behind the Nebraska State Penitentiary. The most common name associated with the cemetery is Grasshopper Hill, but Dairy Hill, Potter's Field, and Pen Field, among others, are also used on occasion. Many of the names of the people beneath this rarely traversed section of earth have been reduced to mere numbers, once held by the men and women who carried them through their time as convicts. Now those numbers, in some cases, are the only means to identify the person buried below. Cemeteries are meant to be peaceful places for family and friends to visit their loved ones after their departure from this world, but Grasshopper Hill has no visitors because the people resting there were unclaimed. In fact, the area is restricted from public access, surrounded by armed prison towers and inaccessible roads. The ones buried there are lost souls on the verge of being forgotten, if they have not been already.

The ghost stories surrounding Grasshopper Hill involve wandering spirits. Figures can be seen crossing the surrounding fields from the top of the hill in the direction of the prison. Occasionally, the apparition has been known to stop, look toward whoever is nearby, and then disappear through the fence line. In addition to emerging from the fields south of the cemetery, other figures can be seen coming from inside of the prison yard and walking toward the cemetery. One particular spirit, who wears a long coat and appears to have no hands, will raise his arm as if to wave and then disappears. People driving along the road west of the cemetery have reported seeing a shiny blue light pass across the road before disappearing into the distance as it makes its way across the field. Others claim that the spirits of murdered prison staff haunt the grounds, trying to find their way home. Sometimes an odd odor emanates from the cemetery and the surrounding fields. Orbs of soft white light also have been seen lingering about the white crosses on the hillside.

• • •

The history of the cemetery contains several intriguing elements. Grasshopper Hill was the final resting place for over one hundred unclaimed people during an 86-year span from 1874 to 1960. According to the inaccurate and incomplete records of the time, the exact number of people and some of their names have been lost. There are currently 133 markers to show the location of a body below, but there are believed to be more than 150 people buried in the cemetery. For several years, graves were marked with headstones containing a piece of paper beneath a glass cover. Over the course of time, many of those glass covers broke and the pieces of paper were destroyed as a result, erasing the identity of the body buried below.

These unidentified bodies will most likely remain without a name or even a number forever, due to poor records management prior to 1960. In any case, most of the people buried in the cemetery had little information associated with them other than their prison sentence and date of death. The fact that the number of people buried in the cemetery is unknown also suggests that some were buried without headstones. Reportedly, only about half of the graves have headstones, leaving the rest to remain anonymous, memorialized with nothing more than a plain cross or not at all.

According to local legend, other people were buried in the cemetery besides inmates, including a family who was seeking refuge in the closest infirmary after becoming ill while traveling. When they reached the penitentiary, they were welcomed inside but later died as a result of their sicknesses. The family was supposedly buried in the cemetery because their identities were unknown. Although no physical evidence exists to prove this particular story is true, the possibility of a family succumbing to illness and being buried in a cemetery known for unclaimed individuals is plausible.

The interesting history of some of the individuals buried on Grasshopper Hill may shed some light on the origins of the stories of ghostly figures seen roaming around the cemetery grounds. On March 14, 1912, inmates John Dowd, Charles Taylor (better known as "Shorty Gray"), and Charles

Morley made their way into the main building of the Nebraska State Penitentiary carrying six-shooters. After motioning to a guard, they were allowed inside where they entered the chapel. Gray and Dowd proceeded to the office of Deputy Warden Charles Wagner where they shot him. Leaving Wagner to die, the men proceeded back into the prison chapel. After hearing the commotion, Usher E. G. Heilman stepped out of his office where he was shot twice. Gray then approached the cage in the turnkey room occupied by Charles Pahl who was hiding against a wall, out of Gray's view. At this point, Guard Thomas Doody entered the chapel after hearing the shots from a cell house west of Wagner's office. After words with Morley, Doody shot at him and was returned with fire from all three convicts. After being shot twice and running low on ammunition, he retreated back to the cell house. Gray then worked on the lock of the turnkey cage by using a homemade explosive of cotton soaked in nitro to remove it. After a flash of light and a loud bang, Gray shook the door a few times until the lock fell to the floor. All three convicts entered the area where Pahl had remained hidden. After stealing the keys, they were met by Warden James Delahunty, who fired at them after emerging from his office, which was next to the cage where the convicts had broken into. He quickly retreated back into his office out of view and when he attempted to fire again, he was met with a bullet hitting him in his right side.

Before collapsing, he was able to pull the trigger again, but still missed the convicts. Once Delahunty was down, the convicts retreated down the hallway toward the main entrance passing the Warden's office where they managed to shoot Delahunty one more time in the chest as he sat upright in the middle of the room. The prison escape ultimately caused the deaths of Warden Delahunty, Deputy Warden Wagner, and Usher Heilman.

After leaving the prison, Dowd, Gray, and Morley—the three convicts—found themselves trudging through blizzard conditions wearing inmate clothing as they made their way toward Omaha. They followed railroad tracks to guide them. Stopping at farms along the way, they forced the occupants to feed them and provide them with ammunition, clothing, and food for travel before leaving. One couple was bound and their phone line was severed, but no one was injured. They also broke into a hardware store and general store in Murdock until they finally ended up at the Blunt farm situated between South Bend and Meadow.

On March 18, four days after killing three men during their escape from the Nebraska State Penitentiary, the three convicts arrived at the Blunt farm. Carmellette Blunt, along with her husband Roy and his brother Lloyd, were in the kitchen when the convicts walked through the door with shotguns aimed at them. Much like the other houses they entered, Carmellette was told to make them breakfast. After being granted permission to retrieve eggs from the chicken coop, Carmellette Blunt stepped outside and ran off. Along the road she found a neighbor passing by in a wagon who took her to his parents' house where she called the sheriff. Realizing that she had fled, the convicts ate quickly and told Roy and Lloyd Blunt to get a wagon ready for them to take. The three convicts made Roy Blunt drive the wagon while they squatted down in the back. They made their way north, passing neighbors who kept their distance.

Groups of law enforcement and locals covered the area as word spread about the location of the men. Approximately 150 to 200 armed men posted themselves at various distances along the escape route while others followed the wagon. Roy managed to bypass several of the groups of men by telling them to hold fire. He told them that as long as they did not shoot, everyone would be safe. After traveling several miles down the road, the convicts' wagon approached Mowinkle schoolhouse. Once the wagon passed the schoolhouse, the first shots were from the direction of a wagon occupied by Chief of Police John Briggs, Sheriff Grant Chase, and Sheriff John C. Trouton, inciting a shootout. Sheriff Gus Hyers from Lincoln, who had been chasing after the men since the escape, road up to get a clear view of the fugitives. In the midst of the gunfire, Roy was hit above his left hip, severing a main artery. After falling into the back of the wagon, Dowd took the reins, while Gray and Morley continued firing on the men surrounding them. Nearing a railroad bridge, in the tenth mile of their pursuit, Gray was shot in the chest and died moments later. Dowd then took his pistol and shot himself in the head. Once Morley realized that he was the only one left, he jumped from the wagon, threw his hands in the air, and surrendered. All three men were brought back to Lincoln, where Morley was tried and sentenced to life in prison. He would spend thirty years behind bars before being released after convincing the prison board that he was a changed man. The bodies of Gray and Dowd lay unclaimed for two weeks before they were sent off to the medical college to be used in an autopsy class. They would later be buried in pine boxes on Grasshopper Hill.

Other notable people buried in the cemetery include Albert Prince, Frank Harold Mackey, and William "Bill" Fitzgerald. On February 11, 1912, one month before the escape and murders committed by Dowd, Gray, and Morley, Albert Prince stabbed and killed Deputy Warden Edward D. Davis with a homemade knife in the Nebraska State Penitentiary chapel. Prince's execution by hanging occurred only a few hundred yards from Grasshopper Hill in a building known as the "hanghouse" on March 21, 1913. Prince was the last person to be hanged as means of execution in the state of Nebraska. After being pronounced dead, Prince was buried in the cemetery.

Another notable person buried on Grasshopper Hill was Frank Harold Mackey who was found guilty in 1932 for shooting and killing a rancher from O'Neill, Nebraska during an attempted robbery. Mackey's accomplice, Lloyd Hammond, signed a confession stating that he had planned the robbery, but that Mackey had shot the man. Hammond was sentenced to twenty-five years and Mackey received a second-degree murder charge and life in prison. Mackey was a Santee Sioux veteran who served in the Marine Corps in World War II. He had been something of a local celebrity for his baseball playing abilities as a pitcher. Mackey was featured in several magazines and was scouted by the Yankees before the criminal conviction landed him in prison.

William "Bill" Fitzgerald was born in California and ended up in Nebraska later in his life. In the 1930s, Fitzgerald was a middleweight boxer known as Billy Ryan who won several titles. After his time as a boxer, Fitzgerald became a bodyguard for actress Jean Harlow until her death in 1937. Fitzgerald also served in the military as a sergeant in the Marines from 1932 to 1942. He was wounded in Gavutu, a small island in the Central Province of the Solomon Islands and was provided a medical discharge. During his time on leave, he was hired to work as a bodyguard for MGM Studios, where he met and began dating actress Gloria Dickson. The couple married in May of 1944.

Less than a year later, Gloria died in a house fire in Hollywood. Fitzgerald would later be arrested for desertion from the military in 1950 while working as a long-haul truck driver. He served his sentence in a military brig in Plattsmouth, New Hampshire and was dishonorably discharged in 1951. In 1955, he married a woman from Darr, Nebraska, but she divorced him after only a month due to the fact that he had been writing bad checks using her bank account. Fitzgerald was sentenced to five years in prison in 1955 for writing a thirty-dollar bad check to Omaha's Castle Hotel, a location known for prostitution. Three years into his sentence, he contracted venereal disease and died. Fitzgerald's body was never claimed; he too was buried on Grasshopper Hill.

Only four women are buried on Grasshopper Hill, two of which have intriguing pasts. Sarah J. (Clinton) Overton was buried there in 1887. She had been incarcerated for murdering her husband; she later committed suicide at the prison. The last woman to be buried in the cemetery was named either Erma Coleman or Evelyn Winters (the name varies according to different records) on June 3, 1930. Coleman was sentenced to two-to-three years on a grand larceny charge in Douglas County. While still in prison, Coleman died during childbirth at the nursing home where female prisoners were sent to give birth. The baby also didn't make it and rumor has it that the child was buried along with her mother in the cemetery after their bodies remained unclaimed.

These lost souls were once living people, left behind to remain for all eternity without visitors, and in some cases even without names to mark their burial spots, doomed to be forgotten.

Narrowing Down the Origins

The ghost stories associated with Grasshopper Hill contain few details that allow for definitive historical connections. Most of the stories involve ghostly figures and odd odors, but contain no dates, names, or even specific areas of the prison or grounds besides the surrounding fields and cemetery. Focusing on the people buried within the small area of land devoted to the unclaimed individuals who were convicted criminals seems to allow for a better understanding of where these stories of apparitions that haunt the graveyard and the surrounding land may have originated.

In 1912, four men were murdered within a one-month period at the Nebraska State Penitentiary, which would have been major news during that time period and would still qualify as major news today. Along with the murders, the prisoners' desperado-type escape spread across the state as the three inmates went from town to town stealing, terrorizing, and eventually ending up in a police chase and shootout that resulted in multiple deaths including the death of an innocent young man. News about these events was widespread, and the fact that the three escapees were on the loose for four days only heightened the fear of local residents.

The interesting histories of the people buried on Grasshopper Hill also lead to intriguing stories that most likely made their way around town. The fact that they were convicts automatically sets them apart from the general public. The people buried in the cemetery had indecorous pasts, some related to violent or horrific events, which could have contributed to stories that eventually became associated with the people who haunt the cemetery grounds. Men with sports-related pasts, murder convictions, Hollywood connections, and possible burials involving a mother and her child only create mystery and intrigue that tends to become the starting point in interesting stories that evolve as they are told over time.

The bottom line is that the people buried on Grasshopper Hill were all unclaimed. Because no one came to take them home to be buried in family plots, they were left to rest alone and in a place that would never be visited by anyone who ever cared for them during their lifetimes. The fact that these people were left behind, some without a name on their gravestone, most likely created the ghost stories that linger amongst the small, white crosses today.

Antelope Park

Near the center of Lincoln, Nebraska, across from the zoo, a golf course, and an ever-evolving neighborhood sits Antelope Park. Once a barren stretch of farmland, the site eventually changed into a bustling central area of town where people spend their afternoons enjoying the attractions the city has to offer. One particular area of the park, however, has a tragedy attached to it. In the southeast corner sits a house where a brutal murder took place over sixty years ago. Ghost stories have since flourished, changing over time to involve multiple apparitions and variations of the history that took place within the park.

The most prominent ghost story involving Antelope Park is that of a woman who appears from the tree line behind the caretaker's house. Several years ago, the area behind the house was fields and farmland. The female apparition is said to emerge from the area, her form is transparent or surrounded by a glowing opaque white light. She has been seen running or walking until she simply disappears. Another female apparition is seen wearing a long flowing white shawl whose feet never touch the ground. She floats around the park near the caretaker's house and into the area near the Veteran's Memorial Garden. Most people have come to know her as the "woman in white." In addition to being seen, she is also known to say the name of the person who is closest to her.

Multiple visitors have reported paranormal experiences. One particular experience involves the double lights near the center of the Veteran's Memorial Garden. One evening, a man in the park was facing toward the area behind the caretakers house when the lights behind him began flickering, causing shadows to cast in the direction he was looking. Believing that the flags on the poles near the lights were passing over the beams, he turned around to find the lights on and the flags hanging still. Several people have reported being touched while in the park. One woman stated that she had her wrist touched and a few moments later felt the grasped of an unseen entity as if another person was trying to hold her hand, but no one else was near her. Another woman said that she felt someone touch the back of her neck. Other reports of touching include being pushed.

One group of visitors who was sitting near the caretaker's house on a picnic table around midnight could smell fire. After searching the area, they found no presence of smoke or flames anywhere in the park. Upon returning to the area where they had originally sat, acorns began falling from a tree above them and the smell of fire came back. They realized the smell was only near the table and nowhere else in the park. Deciding to leave, they walked back to their cars. When they approached one of the vehicles, they found the word fire painted on the concrete. They had not see the message when they originally parked.

One woman, who was holding a recording device while conducting a paranormal investigation, felt her hand suddenly become ice cold. After two hours of attempting to warm up, her hand finally returned back to normal temperature. Fluctuations in temperature occur frequently throughout the park. Some areas feel colder, and abrupt decreases in temperature can be felt in certain areas. Voices are also heard frequently throughout the park. People have reported hearing their own names, whispers, and even screams.

• • •

Antelope Park was not originally intended to be a park. After discovering water along Antelope Creek, the city of Lincoln purchased 41 acres of land owned by W. D. Sager in 1905 for the purpose of constructing sinking wells to provide water for the city. However, only around 30 acres of land provided water and the rest became Antelope Park. The area was officially designated as a park in 1907 after William Jennings Bryan donated a portion of his land, and was expanded in 1915 when W. T. Auld donated another 15 acres. Later the Auld Pavilion and two pillars were erected in honor of his donation. The area was used as a tourist camp in the 1920s where visitors could stay overnight in cabins and tents. A small store was constructed to provide camping gear to patrons. In 1921, Joe Seacrest donated an additional 40 acres and finally in 1932, the city purchased a private enterprise and the land became a city park.

The ghostly apparition known as the "woman in white" can most likely be attributed to the tragic event that took place in the southern end of Antelope Park. A gruesome murder lingered in history, shrouded in mystery and horrific details. Out of such tragic events come stories, full of speculation and distortion that sometimes turn into tales about ghosts. Perhaps the woman who darts out from behind the caretaker's house is that of the woman whose life was tragically taken one winter morning. Understanding the significance of this crime can provide a better understanding of the ghost stories and legends surrounding the park.

Darrel Parker grew up on a farm in western Iowa and went to college at Iowa State University in Ames, Iowa where he majored in forestry. During his sophomore year, he was set up on a blind date with Nancy Morrison from Des Moines, Iowa. They connected immediately and during his senior year, Darrel proposed. They were married on March 20, 1954. While Nancy finished her last year at ISU, Darrel began working in Lincoln, Nebraska after being hired as Lincoln city forester in November. He was 23 years old. Nancy moved in with him after graduating in the summer of 1955. James Ager, head of the park department at the time, moved an older home into Antelope Park. After renovations were completed the Parkers moved in on October

13, 1955. The house was isolated, surrounded by trees, and a block and a half away from the nearest residence.

A month later, an incident occurred that would lead to a string of events that would change both of their lives forever. On November 13, Darrel and Nancy arrived home after spending the evening with friends. They found the dining room window broken and the kitchen table had been moved when someone had entered the home. They found piles of clothes and items strewn throughout the house. Two days later, Ager had a security fence installed by a group of park employees. Unbeknownst to the Parkers and Ager, one of the men on the crew was the person who broke into the house a few nights prior.

On December 14, Darrel left for work, leaving Nancy at their home to finish Christmas cards and run errands before he came home for lunch. He arrived at work around 7:20 a.m. and went about his daily routine as city forester. He left work a little after noon and headed home. When he arrived, he found Nancy's car in the driveway, the windows were still iced over. He could see the shades in their bedroom window were up about half a foot, just like it had been the night of the break-in. Once inside, he found the contents of Nancy's purse scattered across the kitchen counter. He walked through the house to the bedroom where he found a person lying on the bed beneath a quilt with a pillow concealing their head. Darrel pulled the pillow back to find Nancy. She had been strangled with clothesline rope and wire. She was nearly naked, her lip bruised and her left cheek and eye blackened. Her mouth was stuffed with handkerchiefs and her arms were tied behind her back. Nancy had been murdered. Darrel ran from the room and called the police. He also called Ager who arrived to console him. They sat in the living room while police and emergency personnel assessed the scene of the crime. Instead of cutting the rope used to tie Nancy up, police untied the knot, which would later lead to issues during the investigation in regard knot-tying methods used during the murder.

The police departments main lead was a 1949 black Ford two-door seen by nine witnesses parked near the Parker house on Sumner Street. According to reports, the investigation found no evidence of a break-in or robbery. These assessments were later changed to include the fact that there was evidence of a struggle, which ended once Nancy was hit by her attacker. The last time Darrel stepped foot in the house was when he went through with law enforcement to assist in determining if anything had been stolen. He found handkerchiefs and 10 dollars from Nancy's purse missing. Another item was missing as well, one that he did not notice during the walkthrough; a suitcase had been taken from the basement.

On December 15, a man with an extensive criminal record was called in for questioning. His name was Wesley Peery and he, unknown to the investigators, was the man who was on the fence crew and had been the person who had broken into the Parker home a few days prior. Peery was released after taking two lie detector tests. He told the police that he had been sleeping at the time of the murder and had gone to make a key for the trunk of his car, which was a black 1949 Ford. The lie detector tests were brief and administered by two different men who were not polygraph experts. Peery had also taken a tranquilizer before taking the tests. Somewhere along the line, even though the investigation continued to follow the 1949 Ford lead, the focus shifted to Darrel as the main suspect. No physical evidence or witness testimony existed to support this idea.

Darrel returned to Iowa for the funeral, which took place on December 17 in Des Moines. Three days later, Darrel received a phone call to return to Lincoln to help with some new information linked to the case. When Darrel left Iowa, he headed straight for highway patrol headquarters where he was immediately taken into a room, hooked up to a lie detector, and questioned by John Reid, a Chicago Criminologist and lie detector expert. By that evening, Darrel confessed to the murder. According to the confession, he had killed his wife after breakfast because she had refused his advances. Then he went to work and returned home around noon. The next morning, when questioned about his confession, Darrel stated he did recall signing something, but didn't know why he would confess to a crime he did not commit. According to Darrel, when he first entered the interrogation room, Reid told him he looked guilty, told him to sit down, hooked him up to a machine, and proceeded to yell at him. Reid questioned Darrel alone in a windowless room with no other witnesses.

At his arraignment, Darrel pled not guilty. One newspaper reporter stated that Darrel said Reid forced him into a false confession as a result of unorthodox interrogation methods, which included accusations, touching, yelling, depriving him of food, and possibly drugging him when he finally received a sandwich and glass of milk. Reid questioned Darrel from 11:45 a.m. until 3:00 p.m. and then again from 6:15 p.m. until 8:00 p.m. when he confessed.

The trial began on April 9, 1956. The defense attempted to prove Darrel's innocence through witness testimony by people close to him who spoke highly of his character and demeanor. They also used highly respected psychologists, criminologists, and polygraph experts. Two different experts were chosen by the defense to question Darrel using more common practices and both found him to be innocent as a result of their questioning and polygraph. During the trial, autopsy reports were released pegging the time of death to be between 7:20 and 7:40 a.m., the time in which Darrel arrived for work. DNA evidence was found on Nancy and the quilt on the bed, but could not be tested as a result of the lack of technology at the time.

After hearing extensive testimony from multiple people and providing limited evidence, Darrel was found guilty of second-degree murder in May of 1956. He was convicted on the basis of the confession alone. A defense motion for a new trial was overruled on July 2 and the judge sentenced Darrel to life imprisonment as the jury had recommended. Darrel fought hard to reverse the sentence, but the Supreme Court upheld the original conviction. The Eighth District Court, however, ruled in favor of Darrel as a result of lack of evidence to link him to the crime. Darrel remained in prison until 1970 when he was released because of good behavior and the court ruling. He was not exonerated, but was simply placed on parole, with the sentence still looming over his head. At the time of his release, he had spent 13 years of his life in prison.

Wesley Peery, the man who was questioned the day after Nancy was murdered and released, was a repeat criminal. He started off his lifelong criminal record with stealing. Eventually he set a house on fire. At the age of 18, a farmer who lived just outside of Lincoln fostered him. Peery shot the farmer with a shotgun to steal his possessions.

The man survived and Peery was only charged with assault. At 19, Peery stole a vehicle, broke into a bowling alley, and stole a pistol from a car in a parking lot. He would be in and out of prison for the rest of his life. After his release from prison on October 12, 1955, a friend helped him land the job with the city park department without revealing Peery's criminal record. The job would lead him to the Parker's home, where he would meet Nancy in the backyard as she provided cookies to the crew building the fence.

After spending less than a year in prison on a burglary charge, Peery was released from the Nebraska State Penitentiary on April 23, 1957. Not long after he was picked up in Ohio on a robbery and rape charge, which contained several similarities to the Parker murder. The woman in Ohio would live and provide testimony, something Nancy was never able to do. According to Peery, he waited until the woman's husband had left for work and approached the door with a cardboard box. When the woman came to the door, he said that he had a package to deliver. When she opened the door, Peery pulled out a sawed-off shotgun and forced his way inside. He struck her in the face and bound her hands behind her back before raping her. While Peery scoured the house to find items to steal, the woman managed to lock herself in a bathroom. According to the victim's testimony, Peery wore white gloves, only taking them off during the rape and cleaned up the area to get rid of any fingerprints afterwards. Wanting to return to Nebraska, Perry told Ohio detectives he had information about the Parker murder. He specifically told them to ask Lincoln police about a missing suitcase. He wasn't returned and was sentenced to three consecutive 25-year terms. Although his sentence would imply life in prison, Peery was allowed work release in 1975 and returned to Lincoln.

While working at Nebraska Wesleyan University, Peery, along with two accomplices, robbed the Mitzner Coin Shop in Havelock, a small town turned neighborhood a few miles from campus. Peery bound Marianne Mitzner on the toilet while the other two rounded up merchandise. He tied her hands behind her back and left her. Peery helped to grab more goods before heading out to the car where he told the others to wait while he went back inside. Peery went straight into the bathroom and shot Marianne three times. Then he walked back out to the car and went to work for the rest of the day. Peery was sentenced to death for the murder of Marianne.

In the fall of 1978, Peery summoned his attorney to hand over a confession. The handwritten document detailed the murder of Nancy Parker. He provided an accurate layout of the house and could name specific places where Nancy had birthmarks on her body. Peery would never make it to the electric chair; he died as a result of a heart attack in July of 1988. Peery's confession, upon his request, was released after his death.

Years later, Darrel would attempt to retrieve the DNA evidence recovered from the scene of Nancy's murder to be tested, only to find out that all of the evidence was lost. At this point, he could do nothing but accept a pardon he received in 1991 and move on with his life. However, in 2010, two Lincoln lawyers took on Darrel's case, suing the state for wrongful conviction and false imprisonment. They won and Darrel was finally freed from the sentence he was wrongly convicted of for over 50 years. At the age of 80, Darrel was provided a formal apology, exonerated, and given 500,000 dollars.

Narrowing Down the Origins

The most important element of the ghost stories from Antelope Park to consider is the "woman in white" and her proximity in relation to the caretaker's house. The home that still sits within the parks property is the same house where Nancy Parker was murdered in 1955. Although no one else has ever lived in the home since Nancy's death, the structure still remains. Looking at old photos of the home from the newspaper, it shows the same front entrance and distinct windows lining the top half of the house, near the roof. The fact that the stories always include the house is important because of the tragedy that once befell that area. At the time of the murder, the house was secluded, surrounded by trees, and a block and a half away from any other residence. The fact that no one ever includes the house in the stories as a place in which the woman haunts is interesting, but may be a result of lack of accessibility to the home. It may also be due to the fact that the building has been used by the park department for many years and has never been a private residence with the exception of the three months the Parkers lived there. On occasion, people mention a red or purple glowing light in the entryway to the home, providing an ominous vibe. Since no one is allowed to enter the home without authorization, the actual house seems to have little influence on the ghost stories, except for being consistently referenced in relation to where the figure of the woman passes through the tree line and disappears. Whether the ghost is that of the woman who was brutally slain decades ago is up for speculation. Such events seem to resonate and charge an area with energy, but the park has also been in Lincoln for over one hundred years, with numerous generations of people walking across the same soil. The ghost could be anyone, from any time period, but the fact that she is seen so frequently raises the questions of who she is and why she is still in the park. Darrel Parker was wrongfully accused of killing his beloved wife. He spent 13 years of his life in prison, knowing that someone else had committed the crime and was still at large. Wesley Peery confessed to the murder and provided detailed evidence to suggest that he was actually in the house on the morning of December 14, 1955. His gruesome act was left uncharged. We may never know who haunts the area behind the caretaker's house. What is important to remember is that a young woman lost her life, and the man who loved her had to live with that pain and the aftermath of being falsely accused of the crime. The ghost of a woman near the house makes sense in relation to the tragedy that took place and the history surrounding that particular area is important to take note of.

Spring Ranche Bridge

A secluded bridge remains near the once bustling town of Spring Ranche. Nestled deep in the countryside, far from any main road, the town now sits abandoned and left to disappear from the minds of all who once knew such a place existed. The legacy surrounding the old road bridge remains vivid in the minds of those who pass on the ghost stories surrounding a tragic event that occurred there nearly a hundred and fifty years ago.

In 1885, Tom Jones and his widowed sister, Elizabeth Taylor, were hanged from Spring Ranche Bridge and both haunt the place where they were lynched and the cemetery where they were buried. Taylor was known for causing tension with neighbors over her cattle breaching fences and destroying crops on neighboring farms. One afternoon, a man was murdered after being accused of cutting down trees and taking timber from land Taylor claimed she owned. According to witnesses, Taylor was seen running from the area where the murder took place with a shotgun in-hand before disappearing into her home. Fed up with the constant difficulties from the Taylor family, a mob took justice into their own hands. Jones and Taylor were forced out of their home and hanged from Spring Ranche Bridge. As a result of the lynching, a curse was placed on all of those involved causing misfortune and untimely deaths.

Other ghost stories surrounding Tom and Elizabeth involve Spring Ranche Cemetery. According to legend, a tree in the cemetery is a gateway to another realm. Directly across from Tom and Elizabeth's tombstones, on the opposite side of the cemetery, a large tree with a hole in the trunk is said to be the place where the souls of those involved in the lynching were sent after passing on. If anyone touches the tree, they are subjected to the same fate. Many people tried to destroy the tree, but all attempts to do so failed. In one particular case, a man tried to burn the tree and was found dead the next morning in his bed.

According to reports, two ghostly apparitions can be seen hanging from the bridge and oddly shaped mists appear floating near the area where the two where hanged. Others have reported hearing screams, gunshots, chocking sounds, and voices beneath the bridge, as if a group of people is engaged in conversation. A sense of uneasiness is felt when walking across the bridge, and on occasion people have become ill. When driving over the bridge, people have experienced malfunctions with their vehicles including headlights flashing on and off, engines stalling, and radios skipping through stations on their own. The cemetery near the bridge is also known to have ghostly activity. Visitors to the cemetery have reported seeing figures running through the area, shadows, and hearing voices whispering at certain times and talking loudly at others. The area near the tree with the hole is said to be much colder than any other area in the cemetery. The ground has also been reported to always be soft even in the driest parts of the summer, and one headstone in particular is warmer than the others.

• • •

Spring Ranche is all but forgotten. The village that was once a bustling community over a hundred years ago is now vacant with nothing more than the decaying remnants of a few buildings, a cemetery, and a bridge. James Bainter has been given the title of the first permanent settler in Clay County. He built the first homestead in 1863 and the town of Spring Ranche was named after Bainter for the springs that are in close proximity to the area. After Bainter had settled, he began selling potatoes, hay, and other goods by the pound and made a substantial profit. Pawnee and Omaha Indians lived in close proximity of Bainter's home and their relationship with the new settlers in their area was friendly. In the spring of 1864, a group of Sioux hunters arrived. Throughout the summer, they exchanged cash and pelts for goods. However, on the morning of August 9, Bainter was traveling north of his homestead when he saw a Sioux Indian riding toward him. When the Indian caught sight of Bainter, he changed direction and disappeared as he descended toward a ravine. Bainter, feeling uneasy, followed the man to find out where he had gone.

Bainter found the man standing next to his horse looking around. When he saw Bainter, he mounted his horse and quickly rode away, riding on the side of the horse in a position that would keep him safe from any gunshots. The incident aroused suspicion in Bainter, so he rode down to Pawnee Creek and then rode home to warn his wife of an attack.

While Bainter and his wife were preparing at home by getting firearms and ammunition ready, their son arrived to tell them that Indians had attacked Pawnee Ranche. After receiving a description of the men involved, Bainter was sure that one of them was the same man he had seen earlier in the day. The next morning Bainter went to discover what had happened. He found a wagon three miles up the Little Blue River. The occupants told him that Indians had surrounded them the night before and dispersed by morning without any incident. Six miles down the river he found a farm where six men had been killed. Bainter returned home again to find the Indians approaching. He decided to load up his wagon and left for Pawnee Ranche. As the Indians approached the town, a man mounted a horse to get a better view. After two Indians began following the man he turned and fired a shot hitting one of the Indians. In the ensuing battle, three Indian men were killed along with their chief. Bainter arrived home to find his property burned to the ground. Over the next several months, United States troops arrived to help the white settlers by clearing the area of all Native Americans.

After the Sioux raids, the town of Spring Ranche was moved from the north side of the river to the south side before being established in 1870. Bainter opened a general store and an inn. He sold produce, livestock, and other goods, while also providing lodging accommodations for travelers along the Oregon Trail. After the town was established, a mill, cemetery, church, and post office were built, but when the railroad came through in 1886, the town was moved back to the north side of the Little Blue River where the permanent site remains today. The town had several other businesses including two stagecoach stations, a bank, lumberyard, implement store, wagon shop, flour mill, blacksmith shop, barber shop, pool hall, millinery store, molasses mill, broom factory, and a grain elevator.

One of the most significant features of the town's location was its proximity to the Oregon Trail. Part of the trail ran through the area of Spring Ranche. The Oregon Trail is a 2,000-mile trail from Independence, Missouri to Oregon City, Oregon that was used by hundreds of thousands of pioneers in the mid-1800s to trek west across America. The trail ran through Missouri, Kansas, Nebraska, Wyoming, Idaho, and Oregon. The journey was treacherous for travelers and Spring Ranche offered a place to stop to rest and replenish supplies. As a result of the success allotted to the locality of the Oregon Trail, Spring Ranche, at its height, claimed a population of 113 people, but future events would plague the small Nebraska town until its demise. Issues with crops and treacherous weather conditions, especially floods from the Little Blue River every year and tornadoes that tore the town apart caused residents to flee to other areas. In 1885, Spring Ranche would be overshadowed by a treacherous act carried out by a group of men that would stain their reputations for years.

John W. and Margaret Jones immigrated to Missouri, from Wales, in 1860, along with their two children, Elizabeth and Thomas. In 1869, Elizabeth married James A. Taylor and they, along with the rest of the Jones family, moved to Clay County, Nebraska in April of 1872. The Taylors purchased 80 acres of land two miles east of Spring Ranche were they grew crops and raised cattle and hogs. The locals initially welcomed them, but this harmonious period would eventually end. After being confronted by neighboring farmers about their fences being destroyed by the Taylor livestock, James offered to pay for the damages. When Elizabeth found out about his gracious decision, however, she demanded that the farmers provide proof that they were to blame. Eventually, James signed over all property rights to Elizabeth after deciding that she was better at managing the business aspects of the farm. With new power, Elizabeth fought to gain reparations for the money spent by her husband to repair the fences, which in turn created massive tension with the locals.

On May 27, 1882, a local resident saw James riding his horse erratically toward the Little Blue River. James jumped from the horse and began gulping water from the river. When the witness finally caught up with James, he was found lying face down in the water, dead. Although his death was deemed to be natural, most likely a result of untreated diabetes, rumors spread about a possible murder scheme set up by Elizabeth. Evidence came forth showing that she had purchased a large quantity of Paris green, an arsenic-based insecticide used to kill potato bugs. Accusations against Elizabeth in relation to poisoning her husband were widespread amongst the locals because they all knew the Taylors were not potato farmers and the quantity of insecticide she acquired was significantly high in relation to how much she would need for the family garden. Fuel was only added to the flame when her father John Jones suddenly died the following summer.

Several incidents occurred after the death of James Taylor that added to the tension between the Taylor-Jones family and the residents of Spring Ranche. When neighbor boys were found tearing down one of Elizabeth's fences, she sent her two teenage sons to tear down the neighbor's fence. Her sons were caught, tied up, arrested, and released on bond for the crime even though the neighbor's sons were never questioned. The Taylor family became rumored as cattle rustlers and were said to be the only family in town that owned a shotgun. When two of the Taylor's hired hands mysteriously disappeared, the locals began conjuring ideas of what could have happened to them. Finally, Elizabeth accused two men of stealing wood that she claimed was from trees on her land. The accusation would eventually lead to an event that would affect the town for years to come.

In 1884, Elizabeth agreed to allow a man named Edwin "Robert" Roberts, to graze his cattle on a predetermined section of her land. The area chosen was also under a timber grant, but was not part of the grazing agreement that only allowed Roberts to use the land for that purpose. Roberts along with other locals went against this agreement based on the notion that Elizabeth was not using that area to harvest timber, which was a requirement of the grant she was issued. Against Elizabeth's agreement, Roberts along with another man named Joseph Beyer frequently used the area to harvest timber for their own use. On January 8, 1885, Elizabeth's sons, John and William along with their hired hand, saw Roberts and Beyer in a wagon as they made their way out to the area where Roberts was permitted to graze his cattle. Around 2 o'clock in the afternoon, Roberts and Beyer returned with the wagon loaded with timber. The Taylor boys and the hired hand approached Roberts' wagon and accused the two men of stealing. An altercation ensued, which resulted in the horses being spooked causing Beyer to be thrown from the wagon, but Roberts managed to hold tight to the reins. One of the boys then got out of the Taylor wagon, shot Roberts, returned to the wagon, and drove off. Three men who witnessed the event from a neighboring farm ran toward Roberts who they found dead at the scene. The shotgun blast had blown away a significant portion of his face and head. Beyer claimed that one of Elizabeth's sons had fired the shot and another witness stated that William had been the one holding the shotgun. Both boys were promptly arrested and jailed in Hastings.

Rumors spread once again accusing Elizabeth of the murder of Roberts after reports were released stating that she had been seen running into the house with a shotgun. Another rumor spread about her brother, Tom Jones, who had been seen along their fence line carrying a shotgun and a shovel as a hired hand followed behind. When he later returned to the house, he was alone. On March 3, 1885, a group of men surrounded the Taylor home in an attempt to force the occupants out by firing guns into the air. When no one exited the home, the group left without causing any harm to anyone. The following night, the neighbor who fought with Elizabeth over destroyed fences had their barn set on fire. Automatically, Elizabeth was targeted as the culprit.

On the night of March 15, another group of about 15 to 25 men surrounded Tom Jones' home, where Elizabeth had been staying since Roberts was murdered. The mob intended to exact vigilante justice, believing that a trial would take too long and the murderer would not be convicted as a result of lack of evidence. The group called out to Tom and Elizabeth. Instead of complying, the members of the house barricaded the door. After the mob made threats of dropping dynamite down the chimney and through the windows, Tom and Elizabeth complied. Tom exited the house through the window without any firearms and his hands were immediately tied with rope from a mule harness that belonged to Elizabeth. The men then ordered for Elizabeth to come out. She also climbed out the window and her hands were tied as well. Jones and Taylor were taken to an open area near the house. The other people occupying the house at the time the mob arrived were tied up and taken to a nearby residence. Tom and Elizabeth were then told that they were to be hanged for the death of Roberts. At this point, both pleaded for mercy, but they were denied their requests. They were provided time to pray before being taken to the bridge over the Little Blue River. Without hesitation, Jones and Taylor were both placed in nooses. Two different accounts of the way in which the lynching was performed have been recounted. In one rendition, Tom and Elizabeth were taken to the edge of the bridge and shoved off.

In the other version, they were mounted on horses with ropes tied around their necks. Gunshots were fired, spooking the horses and causing them to leave the victims hanging behind. According to reports, the bodies were left on the bridge for several hours. On Sunday morning, a woman crossing the bridge discovered the hanging victims. The bodies were finally cut down when the coroner arrived. A small jury was assembled and the people reported to be involved were interviewed secretly. When each individual testified, they provided little information that would link them to the lynching. Both Tom and Elizabeth were buried in Spring Ranche Cemetery.

After the incident, the community seemed to protect the mob. Five men, who were deemed the leaders of the lynching, were arrested on the charge of first-degree murder. Tom and Elizabeth's mother Margaret testified in court along with another boy who was in the home at the time the mob arrived. Margaret identified one of the men who she had seen the night of the lynching. She claimed that he had entered her house after the hanging to search the house and then left, never taking any precautions to conceal his identity. After identifying one of the members of the mob, the people in the courtroom began pulling out their rifles and revolvers in protest. After hearing all testimonies, all five men were released as a result of insufficient evidence to prosecute.

Narrowing Down the Origins

Most ghost stories are generally devoid of facts because they are usually distorted over time through numerous retellings. The hauntings associated with Spring Ranche Bridge and Spring Ranche Cemetery, however, are curiously similar in nature to the actual events that occurred 1885. The names are the same, the location is accurate, and the tales actually contain a great deal of truth. Of course, the reputation of the Taylor-Jones family is obviously up for interpretation and the opinions of the people who lived in the area around 1885 have most likely been misconstrued and changed over time. However, the rumors associated with the family, especially with Elizabeth, have been documented numerous times throughout the years in various newspapers, interviews, and books. These published reports provide merit to those ideas and can provide a better understanding of the events that occurred resulting in the untimely death of both Elizabeth and Tom, who were potentially innocent of the crime they were accused of. Although the claims about Elizabeth and her neighbors meddling over property rights and destruction of fences are most likely true, other rumors were later proved to be false. For instance, one of the hired men that "mysteriously disappeared" was seen back in Spring Ranche after the lynching, proving that some of the accusations, if not all of them, were not true.

The reason for lynching Tom was never revealed. Although Elizabeth had a bad reputation with the locals, Tom had good report overall. The only odds against him were that he was unmarried, lived with his mother, and was related to Elizabeth. Although he did get along with most people, after the murder of Roberts, suspicions arouse in regard to his involvement in the crime. According to most of the community, Tom was innocent and was simply a victim of a crime he didn't commit. For nearly two years, William and John Taylor remained in jail on the Roberts murder charge. During the hearing, the defense could not provide any solid evidence to convict either teenager. Both were acquitted of all charges. In fact, no charges were ever made for Roberts, Taylor, or Jones.

Finding information linking to the apparitions seen in the cemetery was a much more difficult task. The story involving the tree seems to be a bit far-fetched and most likely is an extension of the curse said to have been placed upon those involved in the lynching. No reports of odd or even tragic deaths in relation to the curse were uncovered, which provides nothing to go off of in regard to those particular stories. The curse is most likely a legend passed down as a result of the lynching and has managed to continue to be told based solely on the tragic events that occurred in 1885. Curses are typically associated with such events, manifesting over time as a means to either justify the actions of those involved by ensuring others that they were punished for their acts or to create a moral for the incident. The cemetery stories are interesting because five people from the Taylor-Jones family are buried there including Elizabeth and Tom. Of course, the apparitions could be those of Elizabeth or Tom, but another interesting aspect of the cemetery is the area designated for those who were never claimed. According to a sign in the cemetery, 29 people are buried in unmarked graves. The lost souls inhabiting the cemetery could also be the ones seen throughout the grounds in search of those who never claimed them after death.

The incident fueled more fire to an already tense community. The lynching seemed to be a decision that haunted those involved for years. The fact that no proof was ever presented to charge anyone with the murder of Roberts, would have quite possibly provided the dropping of any charges toward Elizabeth. The fact that Tom was also lynched shows how extreme the town's hatred was for the family. Narrowing down the origins isn't difficult when most of the facts are still in the ghost stories, but that doesn't change the importance of the apparitions still seen lurking around the bridge and cemetery. Most of all, it doesn't change the fact that two people were lynched nearly 150 years ago with little evidence to prosecute them in the first place, especially since the individual who was reported to have pulled the trigger that killed

Roberts was never even charged. What happened on Spring Ranche Bridge will echo in time for all eternity. Elizabeth Taylor was the only recorded woman ever lynched in the State of Nebraska. The death of both individuals will be on the hands of those involved forever, whether their names are public or not. Elizabeth and Tom's spirits still linger near the place they were sent to die for a crime they may have never even committed.

Nebraska State Capitol

The most notable building in Nebraska is the Nebraska State Capitol. The building towers over the city of Lincoln as a central landmark. Buildings with a long history are often subject to ghost stories, and the Nebraska State Capitol is among those structures. Standing as a pinnacle of achievement to the success of Nebraska, the Capitol houses the state government, displays historical murals and depictions of life in the Midwest, and exhibits some of the finest and unique architectural design in the United States. Surrounded by the city of Lincoln, the Capitol building embodies the pride of the plains, visible for miles in all directions. Through the halls, echoes of the past can still be heard, apparitions are seen, and the presence of those who have died within the buildings walls are said to remain.

Several ghosts are said to haunt the Nebraska State Capitol. Tragic accidents seem to cause most of the hauntings that have been recorded. Three different versions of a similar story involve a man falling to his death from some of the highest points of the building. The most common story involves a male inmate falling from the dome during the Christmas season. In the 1960s, the dome was covered in Christmas lights each year, shining brightly throughout the month of December. The task of hanging decorations at 400 feet, atop a smooth surfaced dome, would have to be taken on by someone unafraid of heights. Inmates from the Nebraska State Penitentiary were asked to volunteer each year and in return they would receive praise for taking on such a dangerous job and could use their willingness as an appeal to the parole board the next time the inmate was up for possible release. One night, after everyone else had left the building, a prison guard, a maintenance worker, and an inmate who had volunteered to string up the lights, made their way up to the dome. After strapping the inmate into a harness and securing all the proper ropes and material needed to keep the man safe, he made his way out onto the dome. Two different versions of the story are told about what happened next. The first tells of the inmate succumbing to overwhelming fear brought on after realizing how high up he was, causing him to have a heart attack and fall to his death. The second story involves the inmate slipping, losing his grip, and falling to his death. In both instances, the inmate's screams echoed through the city.

Another story involves a man who was visiting the Nebraska State Capitol to explore the architecture and learn about the history. On an afternoon in the 1950s, the man ascended the spiral staircase up to the observation decks. While on the stairs, he leaned over and either became overwhelmed with dizziness or lost his balance, falling 14 stories to his death. No one witnessed what happened and the reasoning for his fall remains unknown.

The final story involving a falling death was that of a Nebraska State Capitol worker. One afternoon, a maintenance worker found a bulb had burned out above one of the observation decks. After retrieving all the tools needed to finish the replacement, he got on the elevator and made his way up to the 14th floor. Once at the top, he organized his tools and began the process of replacing the bulb. As he reached up to secure the bulb into the socket, the worker slipped and fell to this death.

Another area of the building that has reported hauntings is the law library. A woman is said to linger in the area. She is particularly known for touching male visitors. One man claimed that he was helped locate the light switch in the darkness of the room. He believed that the touch was that of a woman. Another incident involving a female entity was from a worker repairing the ceiling. Upon entering the work site, he found his tools had been moved across the room. Since no one else was allowed in the area after he left the previous evening, he simply believed that he had been mistaken and had moved the tools. While working on the repairs, a splash of chemicals landed in his eyes, temporarily blinding him. As he tried to make his way down to the main part of the building, he felt the presence of someone guide him to safety. He believed it was the woman from the library he had heard stories about.

The most commonly reported supernatural occurrence is hearing a man sobbing while riding the elevator or while standing on the southwest side of the observation deck. Disembodied voices and screaming can be heard throughout the building, but especially on the observation decks. Footsteps and loud banging noises are also heard frequently throughout the hallways and stairways. There are reports of books found scattered across the floor, objects moving on their own, doors and windows slamming shut, workers tools being moved across the room, and the elevator moving up and down on its own. People have also felt as if they are being watched. One of the most incredible experiences, however, is that people have seen an apparition or misty form while standing on the steps halfway up to the 12th floor. The form is seen falling down to the first floor. Others have reported seeing a black mass in various stairways.

• • •

Several incidents have occurred at the Nebraska State Capitol involving injuries and even death, but the construction and history of the building can provide several other reasons why ghostly figures are seen wandering the halls and stairways. Construction of the first Nebraska State Capitol occurred between 1867 and 1868. The original building was two stories with a central cupola. The building materials and poor construction resulted in quick deterioration. Another Capitol was built in 1888, but suffered the same issues as the first, which resulted in the plans to build a third, much more solid and long lasting Capitol building. Through a nationwide design competition, Architect Bertram Grosvenor Goodhue was chosen for the final plans. The Capitol was built over a ten-year period, from 1922 to 1932 and cost the State of Nebraska just under $10 million dollars. Goodhue chose sculptor Lee Lawrie for the tile, mosaic designer Hildreth Meier as the thematic consultant for inscription and symbolism, and Hartley B. Alexander to decorate the building. In addition to the main structure of the building, four interior courtyards were added, and a bronze figure known as the "Sower" was placed atop the dome. Today, the Nebraska State Capitol is the seat of government for the State of Nebraska. The Capitol houses the primary, executive, and judicial offices of Nebraska and the Nebraska Legislature, which is the only state unicameral legislation in the United States.

Some of the incidents and events that have occurred at the Nebraska State Capitol may allow for a better understanding of the ghost stories associated with the building. Between 1961 and 1968, the dome of the Capitol was decorated with a crown of white Christmas lights. From mid-December to January 1st, the lights could be seen for miles in all directions atop the building. Although inmate workers were allowed to clean and paint the dome in 1961, State of Nebraska employees were responsible for stringing the lights and maintaining the bulbs that would burn out or burst on account of the weather. Workers would hoist long strings of lights onto the dome by use of cables, ropes, and pulleys from the 15th floor and fasten them to the base of the "Sower." In 1963, a worker actually lost his footing and was suspended for a short period of time, after his ropes became tangled, but he did not fall or die. After the incident the worker decided to terminate his position because of the risk. The lights were discontinued in 1968 as a result of lack of funding. Maintaining the lights was too costly and wooden spreaders on the light strings and the bursting of bulbs damaged the gold finish on the dome.

Deaths have occurred within the building, and when looking at the ghost stories associated with Nebraska State Capitol, two particular instances seem to reflect on how the stories associated with the building may have received their origins. On February 11, 1911, a night watchman fell to his death from the third story of the Capitol. Two theories arose from the incident as to whether or not the man fell or if he was thrown over. Another worker in the building found the watchman's lifeless body, surrounded by a pool of blood, as he descended the south corridor stairs after leaving his office. The watchman had landed in front of the Governor's office on the main level. Once the body was found, the watchman's son, who was in the building at the time, admitted that his father had drank a considerable amount of alcohol earlier in the evening. An autopsy indicated the cause of death was a fractured skull, but there were other cuts on his body that appeared to have nothing to do with the skull injury, which indicated that a sharp object such as a knife may have been used to inflict those wounds. Although at the time the police could not pinpoint a motive, the investigators and coroner believed that the man had been attacked and thrown over. Other night watchmen were working in the area only about 100 feet away from the spot where the man was believed to have fallen. Although the other watchmen were in close proximity, no one heard the man scream, but his footsteps were heard walking down the corridor just before he fell. Without any witnesses present to determine the cause of the fall, the death was ruled as an accidental fall due to intoxication.

Another man plunged to his death on November 13, 1945. The man was originally from Filley, Nebraska and, at the time of his death, was the Chief Dairy and Milk Inspector for the City of Lincoln Health Department. He was a University of Nebraska graduate from the college of agriculture and was a World War I veteran, who had received the Purple Heart after being wounded in his back by shrapnel. The man fell to his death after he leaped or lost his footing while on the northwest corner of the observation deck on the 14th floor. After falling 250 feet, the man plunged through the skylight and into one of the fourth-floor offices of the State Assistance Department, where he landed face down on a desk and died instantly. Two women were working in the area at the time, and they described the sound of the crash as if an explosion had gone off. Although two other visitors were on the observation deck at the time, no eyewitnesses visibly saw how the initial fall occurred. The man had not left a note behind for his family, indicating that the fall may not have been a suicide. Aside from taking his own life, the fall could have been a result of a condition the man received after fighting overseas. As a result of his injury from WWI, the man was known to have dizzy-spells, but according to his physician had been in good health at the time of the fall. Due to the lack of witnesses and the absence of a note, the death was ruled accidental, but the truth was never discovered

Narrowing Down the Origins

One reason for the number of stories revolving around a person falling to their death in the building could be attributed to the sheer size and architecture of the Nebraska State Capitol. The building is tall and slender, almost like an enormous tower, and the smooth dome, observation decks, and spiral staircase cause a sense of vertigo and fear related to the sensation of falling. The building is open to the public year-round and visitors are allowed to venture to the top to catch a view of the city from Lincoln's highest structure. The history related to the two people who have fallen to their death in the building can also be attributed to the recurring ghost stories associated with a sobbing man who remains near the southwest side of the building. The stories associated with the worker falling while fixing a light bulb, could be linked to the worker who died in 1911. The fact that an inmate is generally the person who fell while putting lights on the dome is interesting, since actual staff performed the job. The use of inmates in the story can be linked to the fact that they did work inside and around the Capitol, and some even cleaned and painted the dome in the 1960s. All of the ghost stories, with the exception of the woman in the library, have some truth to them and could have easily started off as an actual event distorted over generations of retelling.

The presence and significance the Nebraska State Capitol has for the state allows for stories to be told over and over, in various different ways. The prominence of such a building can create tales that stand the test of time. Daily visitations by the public, the use of the building for the state government, and the rich history associated with the building allows for those stories to continue to thrive. Accessibility and operation of the building allows for the echoes of the past to remain open to the public to experience firsthand.

Bibliography

20th and Washington

"A. F. Barstow Shot in Own Door Yard." *The Sunday State Journal*, 23 Jan. 1921, p. 1.

"Adrian Barstow Is Killed." *The Lincoln Sunday Star*, 23 Jan. 1921, p. 1.

"Barstow Inquest Is Tuesday Night." *The Lincoln Daily Star*, 25 Jan. 1921, p. 1.

"End of Many False Trails." *Sunday State Journal*, 30 Jan. 1921, p. 6.

"First Theory Abandoned." *The Nebraska State Journal*, 28 Jan. 1921, p. 5.

"Hyers Is Confident." *The Lincoln Daily Star*, 26 Jan. 1921, p. 1.

"Matson Seeks Suggestions." *The Nebraska State Journal*, 29 Jan. 1921, p. 7.

"Murderer Still a Mystery." *The Lincoln Daily Star*, 24 Jan. 1921, pp. 1-5.

"Narrowly Escaped Motor Car Crash." *The Nebraska State Journal*, 27 Jan. 1921, p. 1.

"Police Interview Barstow's Friends." *Lincoln Daily News*, 25 Jan. 1921, p. 1.

"Wall of Mystery Fronts Detectives." *Lincoln Daily News*, 31 Jan. 1921, p. 1.

Wilderness Park

"Caught a Fiend." *The Nebraska State Journal*, 11 Aug. 1884, p. 1.

"Charred Bones." *The Nebraska State Journal*, 11 Aug. 1884, p. 1.

"Davis Found Guilty." *Lincoln Evening News*, 28 Nov. 1895, p. 1.

"Death by Fire." *The Nebraska State Journal*, 10 Aug. 1884, p. 1.

Fisher, George. "Gone Are the Days - Epworth Park." *The Nebraska State Journal*, 19 Sept. 1943, p. 25.

"Is Davis the Man?" *The Evening News*, 11 Aug. 1984, p. 1.

"Last Edition. Begins the Quest." *The Evening News*, 11 Aug. 1884, p. 1.

"Last Edition. A Dastardly Deed." *Lincoln Evening News*, 10 Aug. 1884, p. 1.

McKee, Jim. "Epworth Park." *Remember When... Memories of Lincoln*, J & L Lee Co, 1998, p. 17.

"Rock Island Wrecker Will Get Commutation." *Lincoln Evening News*, 6 May 1905, p. 1.

"Thirteen Lives Are Sacrificed." *Lincoln Weekly Call*, 10 Aug. 1884, p. 1.

"Today's Events." *The Nebraska State Journal*, 1 Nov. 1916, p. 13.

Vint, Tom. "Touch of Wilderness for Lincoln's Enjoyment." *Lincoln Journal Star*, 9 Sept. 1973, p. 34.

Seven Sisters Road

"A Flash in the Pan." *The Nebraska State Journal*, 18 Jan. 1887, p. 7.

"A Mysterious Murder." *The Nebraska State Journal*, 1 May 1886, p. 1.

"Child Murderers." *Lincoln Daily News*, 4 May 1886, p. 4.

Dale, Raymond Elmer. *Otoe County Pioneers: a Biographical Dictionary*. Lincoln, Neb.: [s.n.], 1961. 2670-2671. Print.

"Doomed to Die." *The Nebraska State Journal*, 9 Dec. 1886, p. 1.

"Guilty of Murder." *Lincoln Daily News*, 8 Dec. 1886, p. 4.

"Had Their Trip for Nothing." *The Nebraska State Journal*, 26 Mar. 1887, p. 1.

"Hung By a Mob." *Lincoln Daily News*, 25 July 1887, p. 4.

"Not Guilty." *The Nebraska State Journal*, 20 Nov. 1887, p. 3.

"On Trial for Life." *The Nebraska State Journal*, 17 June 1887, p. 8.

Potter, James E. "'Wearing the Hempen Neck-Tie': Lynching in Nebraska, 1858-1919," Nebraska History 93 (2012): 138-153

"Shellenberger's Lynching." *The Nebraska State Journal*, 29 July 1887, p. 1.

"State House Notes." *Daily Nebraska State Journal*, 23 Mar. 1887, p. 7.

"The Murder Trial." *Lincoln Daily News*, 16 June 1887, p. 4.

"The Shellenberger Case." *The Nebraska State Journal*, 1 Dec. 1886, p. 1.

"The Shellenberger Trial." *The Nebraska State Journal*, 16 June 1887, p. 7.

"The State." *The Daily State Journal*, 16 Dec. 1880, p. 2.

Bloody Mary

"Elderly Woman Uses Shotgun, Kills Man." *The Lincoln Star*, 30 Oct. 1966, p. 28.

Hudson, Joe. "Arsonist's Flame Ends Horror Tale." *The Lincoln Star*, 11 Aug. 1977, p. 11.

"Mary A. Partington." *Lincoln Journal*, 16 June 1979, p. 4.

"Partington Case Cited." *Lincoln Journal Star*, 5 Nov. 1966, p. 22.

Partington, Joseph C. "Partington History." *The Lincoln Star*, 25 Aug. 1977, p. 4.

Partington, Mary. "Assaults." *Lincoln Journal Star*, 1 Oct. 1966, p. 4.

Reinehr, Frances Grace. *Bloody Mary: Gentle Woman*. Foundation Books, 1989.

Stevenson, Jim. "Elderly Woman Slays Intruder." *The Lincoln Star*, 27 Oct. 1966, p. 25.

Tillinghast, Bill. "Intruder Is Slain by Elderly Woman." *Lincoln Journal Star*, 26 Oct. 1966, p. 1.

Barnard Park

Buck, Renee. "Early History of Fremont, Nebraska." *History of Fremont*, The Pathfinder Press, 2000, www.usgennet.orgusa/ne/county/dodge/fremonthist.htm.

"Early Nebraskan Dies of Old Age." *The Lincoln Daily Star*, 23 Oct. 1910, p. 3.

"First House in Fremont." *Omaha Daily Bee*, 9 Mar. 1890, p. 16.

"Founder of Fremont Dead." *The Nebraska State Journal*, 22 Oct. 1910, p. 11.

"Fremont Fifty Years Old." *Omaha Daily Bee*, 7 Jan. 1907, p. 2.

"History & Culture." *National Parks Service*, U.S. Department of the Interior, 2018, www.nps. gov/mopi/learn/historyculture/index.htm.

"Hitch in Negotiations." *The Lincoln Daily Star*, 8 July 1905, p. 3.

"Mormon Trail Is Located." *Lincoln State Journal*, 8 Aug. 1925, p. 8.

National Register of Historic Places. Barnard Park Historic District. Fremont, Dodge County, Nebraska, National Register #90001053.

Real-McKeighan, Tammy. "Ridge Cemetery Has Seen Many Changes over the Years."

Fremont Tribune, 25 Aug. 2012, fremonttribune. com/news/local/ridge-cemetery-has-seen-many-changes-over-the-years/ article_761c0220-ee6a-11e1-8e9d-0019bb2963f4.html.

Rickerl, Stephen. "Fall Festival Will Highlight Haunted Fremont." *Fremont Tribune*, 12 Oct. 2013, fremonttribune.com.

Norfolk Regional Center

"Asylum Fire Fighters." *Norfolk Weekly News Journal*, 26 May 1905, p. 6.

"Asylum in Ruins." *The Nebraska State Journal*, 24 Sept. 1901, pp. 1–2.

"Asylum Wiped Out." *The Lincoln Evening News*, 23 Sept. 1901, pp. 1–6.

"Attendant at Norfolk Asylum Fatally Burned." *The Lincoln Daily Star*, 25 Apr. 1907, p. 3.

"Death Caused by a Scuffle." *Nebraska State Journal*, 8 June 1915, p. 6.

"Doctor Is Fatally Shot at Hospital in Norfolk." *Lincoln Journal Star*, 26 Oct. 1996, p. 1.

Hartmann, Klaus, and Les Margolin. "The Nebraska Asylum for the Insane, 1870-1886," Nebraska History 63 (1982): 164-182

"Hospital in Ruins." *Omaha Daily Bee*, 24 Sept. 1901, pp. 1–2.

"Hospital Needs $90,000." *The Norfolk Weekly News*, 14 Dec. 1906, p. 3.

"Inmate of Norfolk Asylum Killed Himself with Razor." *Nebraska State Journal*, 27 Dec. 1906, p. 3.

"Inmate State Hospital at Norfolk Ends Life."
    Nebraska State Journal, 26 Feb. 1929, p. 3.

Laughlin, Harry Hamilton. *Eugenical Sterilization
    in the United States*. Psychopathic
    Laboratory of the Municipal Court of
    Chicago, 1922.

McKee, Jim. "Nebraska's Regional Centers Got
    Their Starts in the 1880s." *Lincoln Journal
    Star*, 29 Feb. 2004, p. 24.

"Norfolk Hospital for Insane Was Opened in
    1888." *The Lincoln Star*, 21 May 1980.

"Norfolk Patient Commits Suicide." *The Lincoln
    Daily Star*, 4 May 1907, p. 5.

"Patient Burns to Death." *Lincoln Evening
    Journal*, 27 Feb. 1933, p. 6.

"Probe to Be Made in Norfolk Death." *Lincoln
    Daily News*, 7 June 1915, p. 1.

Schmeckpeper, Sheryl. *Norfolk, Nebraska*.
    Arcadia Publishing, 2000.

"Scuffle Leads to Inmate's Death." *The Lincoln
    Daily Star*, 29 May 1915, p. 1.

"State Officials Will Endeavor to Estimate Damages of Norfolk Asylum Fire." *The Lincoln Evening News*, 26 Sept. 1901.

"The Jury Finds That an Employee at the Norfolk Asylum Died From the Effects of an Abortion." *Nebraska State Journal*, 8 Feb. 1889, p. 3.

"The Lincoln Evening News." *The Lincoln Evening News*, 29 May 1911, p. 4.

Winters, Gordon. "State Will Close Norfolk Regional Center." *The Lincoln Star*, 21 May 1980, p. 36.

Grasshopper Hill

"Actress Gloria Dickson to Marry Bill Fitzgerald." *Lincoln State Journal*, 4 May 1944, p. 6.

"Are Scouring Country for Fleeing Convicts." *The Lincoln Daily Star*, 15 Mar. 1912, pp. 1–5.

"Bloody Battle Marks Last Effort to Break Through Lines to Freedom." *Lincoln Daily News*, 18 Mar. 1912, p. 1.

Christianson, Gale E. *Last Posse: a Jailbreak, a Manhunt, and the End of Hang-'Em-High Justice.* The Lyons Press, 2001.

"Convicts Actions at Farmers Home." *The Lincoln Daily Star*, 19 Mar. 1912, p. 4.

"Death Ends Flight of Convict Murderers." *The Lincoln Daily Star*, 18 Mar. 1912, p. 1.

"Desperadoes at Pen Take Warden's Life." *The Nebraska State Journal*, 15 Mar. 1912, pp. 1–3.

"Gloria Dickson Film Actress Dies in Blaze." *The Lincoln Star*, 11 Apr. 1945, p. 2.

"Trail of Murderers Now Leads to Omaha." *The Lincoln Daily Star*, 17 Mar. 1912, pp. 1-6.

Antelope Park

Campbell, Roy, and Virgil Falloon. "Murder Mystery Deepens." *The Lincoln Star*, 15 Dec. 1955, p. 1.

Falloon, Virgil. "Defense Lie Test 'Proves Innocence'." *The Lincoln Star*, 11 Jan. 1956, p. 1.

Hicks, Nancy. "Attorney's Say Peery Enjoyed Describing Details of Murders." *The Lincoln Star*, 29 Nov. 1988, pp. 1–8.

"Husband Finds Body." *Lincoln Evening Journal*, 14 Dec. 1955, p. 1.

McKee, Jim. "Antelope Park." *Remember When... Memories of Lincoln*, J & L Lee Co, 1998, p. 20.

McKee, Jim. "Antelope Park Becomes Jewel in System's Crown." *Lincoln Journal Star*, 26 Nov. 1996, p. 26.

"Parker Petition On File." *Lincoln Evening Journal and Nebraska State Journal*, 6 June 1962, p. 8.

"Police Check 'Lots of Leads' in Murder Case." *Lincoln Evening Journal*, 16 Dec. 1955, p. 1.

Randol, Elwood. "1st Degree Murder Charge Filed Here Against Parker." *Lincoln Evening Journal*, 22 Dec. 1955, p. 1.

Randol, Elwood. "Parker in Pen After Pleading Innocent To 1st Degree; to Face Jury." *Lincoln Evening Journal*, 23 Dec. 1955, p. 1.

Salter, Peter. "$500k Wrongful Conviction Suit Filed in '55 Murder Case." *Lincoln Journal Star*, 20 July 2011.

Salter, Peter. "A Killer Confesses to '55 Lincoln Murder: 'I Put the Shotgun on Her'." *Lincoln Journal Star*, 15 Jan. 2011.

Salter, Peter. "Book on '55 Lincoln Murder Reopens Questions, Wounds." *Lincoln Journal Star*, 18 Dec. 2010.

Salter, Peter. "Evidence Vanishes in Murder Case." *Lincoln Journal Star*, 18 Dec. 2010.

Salter, Peter. "State Apologizes, Pays $500k to Man in 1955 Wrongful Conviction." *Lincoln Journal Star*, 31 Aug. 2012.

Strauss, David L. *Barbarous Souls*. Northwestern University Press, 2010.

Spring Ranche Bridge

"A Disgraceful Affair." *Omaha Daily Bee*, 21 May 1885, p. 4.

"Another Murder: Robert Roberts the Victim of a Quarrel in Clay County." *The Nebraska State Journal*, 10 Jan. 1885, p. 1.

"Double Lynching." *Daily Nebraska State Journal*, 17 Mar. 1885, p. 1.

"Examination of the Lynchers." *The Daily State Journal*, 8 Apr. 1885, p. 6.

History of Spring Ranch, 1870-1990. Spring Ranch Homemakers Extension Club, 1990.

McKee, Jim. "Lynching of Taylor, Jones in Clay County." *Lincoln Journal Star*, 3 Sept. 2006, p. 22.

Swanson, Hjalmar A. *Clay County, Nebraska Past and Present...Yesterday and Today*. Fort Wayne Public Library, 1983.

Terrill, Dean. "Lynchings Disremembered." *Lincoln Journal Star*, 17 Mar. 1985, p. 1.

"The Citizens' Meeting." *Sutton Register*, 22 Mar. 1885, p. 8.

"The Clay County Lynching." *Hastings Gazette Journal*, 19 Mar. 1885, p. 3.

"The Lynchers: Five Men Arrested as Leaders of the Spring Ranche Mob." *The Nebraska State Journal*, 26 Mar. 1885, p. 1.

"The Taylor Boys Acquitted." *Hastings Gazette Journal*, 23 May 1886, p. 4.

Thompson Hall, Edith. "History Told by a Child Grown Old." *Lincoln Sunday Journal and Star*, 3 July 1966, p. 43.

Woolsey, George, and Shirley Aksamit. *The Story of Clay County "Best in Nebraska"*. 1969.

Nebraska State Capitol

"427 White Light Bulbs to Shine on Capitol Dome." *The Lincoln Star*, 13 Dec. 1961, p. 1.

"An Accident?" *Lincoln Daily Star*, 14 Feb. 1911, p. 5.

"Coroner's Jury Probes Death." *Lincoln Daily Star*, 13 Feb. 1911, p. 10.

"Kohler Falls to Death from Capitol Tower." *The Lincoln Star*, 14 Nov. 1945, pp. 1–8.

"Man 'Domefounded' for Awhile." *Lincoln Evening Journal*, 27 Nov. 1963, p. 8.

Naugle, Ronald C., and James C. Olson, "Establishing the State Government." *History of Nebraska*, 3rd ed., University of Nebraska Press, 1997, p. 150.

"Nebraska State Capitol." *Historic Capitol Location Sites and Buildings – Building History - Nebraska State Capitol*, Capitol Group, 2018, capitol.nebraska.gov/.

"No Christmas Lights for Statehouse Dome." *The Lincoln Star*, 11 Dec. 1968, p. 17.

"Top Capitol Spot to Pen Inmates." *Lincoln Evening Journal*, 5 June 1961, p. 5.

"Watchman Found Dead in Capitol Building." *Lincoln Daily Star*, 12 Feb. 1911, pp. 1–4.

"Youth Aided Pen Escapee." *Lincoln Evening Journal*, 1 Sept. 1961, p. 12.

Acknowledgments

First of all, I would like to thank my beautiful partner Ashton, for listening to me ramble on and on about the amazing stories I uncovered while conducting research for this book. She has stood by me through long nights and early mornings and I appreciate everything she does for me. I want to thank my family for all of their support—my mother and father for always standing behind my decisions and being there when I need them, my brother for listening to me as if I were the greatest storyteller in the world, Emma for wanting to read my stories when I finish them, and my grandmother and grandfather for being the heart and soul of our family and filling our ears with tales of their childhood, jokes, and folklore. I love you all.

I want to thank University of Nebraska-Lincoln professor Dr. Beverley Rilett for listening to my ideas for this book as an independent study course project and for supporting my decision to take on such a rewarding and challenging project. Thank you C Balta for creating such an amazing cover design and being an amazing friend. Thank you Nebraska State Historical Society and Archives and Special Collections for providing historical documents and information. Thank you Lincoln Journal Star for the abundance of articles I had the privilege of reading through. Thank you Paul Royster for teaching me how to format a book. Thank you

Lauren Shoemaker for taking the time out of your day to find newspaper articles and pamphlets that assisted in my research. Thank you Lisa O'Neill for sharing the stories you uncovered and a location that became a new chapter. Thank you Paranormal Research and Investigation Nebraska Team for sharing your stories and taking me along on an investigation. Thank you to everyone who shared their personal ghost stories that found their way into the pages of this book. Thank you Nebraska for being the place I call my home.

Thank you to all the storytellers who filled my ears with ghost stories and the history connected to them that allowed this book to become a reality. And thank you to all of my family and friends for supporting the development of this book, for telling the ghost stories that have excited my imagination, and for believing in me.

Disclaimer

The author or anyone affiliated with this book does not support trespassing in order to visit haunted locations. Before visiting, ensure that permission and/or permits are received in order to avoid destruction of property, trespassing on privately owned land, or altering landmarks. The above-mentioned offenses if violated are punishable by law and help to ensure the preservation of these places. Check the hours of operation, city and county regulations, and rules before visiting. Learning about the history, tales, and folklore of Nebraska, especially about the people who once walked across the same soil, can create a better understanding of one's community, local history, and the importance of the people who shaped their towns and cities. Please do not break the law and please do not disrespect the dead or the living that watch over or own the areas included in this book.

About the Author

Tayden Bundy was born and raised in Lincoln, Nebraska. He graduated from the University of Nebraska in 2018 with a Bachelor of Arts degree in English and history. Over the summer of 2017, he was an intern for *Prairie Schooner*. His work has been published in *Illuminations, Laurus Magazine,* and *The Airgonaut. Beyond Lincoln: A History of Nebraska Hauntings* is his first book.